Conversations
with
an
Immigrant

Mariorafols Menezes

ISBN-13: 978-1-9991091-0-3

Cover Design: Muhammad Awais

Text Design & Copyediting: Marianne Thompson

TABLE OF CONTENTS

Acknowledgment i

Foreword iii

Chapter 1: Arrival 1

Chapter 2: Rendezvous 7

Chapter 3: Frustration 19

Chapter 4: Mentoring 27

Chapter 5: Mindset 35

Chapter 6: Day One 47

Chapter 7: Beliefs 59

Chapter 8: Inspiration 69

Chapter 9: Growth 79

Chapter 10: Giving 89

Chapter 11: Forgiving 97

Chapter 12: Success 107

About the Author 115

Book Recommendations 116

ACKNOWLEDGEMENT

I had dreamed of writing a book since my early twenties, but always thought I'm not ready or I didn't have all the information I needed to begin writing it. God, however, has amazing ways to create life experiences that pushed me out of my comfort zone to write this book. I thank Jesus for giving me the incentive.

This book would not have been possible without the teachings from gurus like Jim Rohn and Tony Robbins. I have immersed myself listening, reading, and striving to live by their words. Most of Dave's mentoring lessons in this book are a reflection of their guidance.

Writing this book has been a challenge, but Rebecca Cheung, my coach and mentor, helped me realise my dream of completing this book and I thank her.

I don't know what I would have done without my wife, Anna. Without her encouragement and persistence, this book might have been just a dream.

FOREWORD

Most immigrants coming to Canada go through five stages while settling down in that country. Understanding the process of integrating in this country will provide you with the courage and confidence that you are not alone. You will learn that the life experiences you are going through are no different than most other immigrants who come here. Every immigrant has a personal story to tell – glorious or painful. The secret to settling fast and settling well in Canada is to refuse and refrain from accepting another person's negative story as your own.

The five stages that an immigrant experiences when they come to Canada are:

1. Anxiousness
2. Resistance
3. Endurance
4. Stability
5. Prosperity

This book reveals the philosophy and focus that will reduce the time you and your family spend in the first three stages – Anxiousness, Resistance, and Endurance, while settling in Canada so that you experience stability and prosperity - which has been and will remain your goal that you planned for before moving to Canada.

There are many who come to Canada and go back to their home country disappointed and dejected. Others return, while some others move to another country in Europe, the U.S., or the Australian subcontinent.

A significant number of prospective immigrants consider moving to Canada as a means to alleviate the troubles and difficulties they experience in their home country. Though there is some truth to this, it would be naïve to believe that there will be less or no difficulties when you come to Canada. Starting a new life in Canada brings with it a different set of changes, challenges, and learnings which you need to embrace, endure, and embody as you progress toward becoming a citizen.

This book is a fictional representation of an immigrant's life in Canada. It is written to help you as a new immigrant to embrace the typical experiences most new immigrants face when they start life in Canada. The experiences of the new immigrant shared in this book embodies life experiences that you may relate to if you are already here, or help you anticipate the kind of experiences you may experience when you come to Canada. Most new immigrants get conditioned to interpret their early experiences in Canada negatively. *Conversations with an Immigrant* provides an encouraging outlook to make things work to your advantage.

This book showcases immigrants and aspirants a flavour of life in Canada, and a chance to contemplate their decision before they immigrate to this country. This book attempts to inspire immigrants to excel personally and contribute collectively by anchoring their determination and maintaining a progressive mindset. The thinking shared in the story is a concoction of philosophies and ideas shared by great achievers and trendsetters of our times. Most of the practical thought processes woven into the story are a blend of contemporary self-help and conscious manifestation.

I have greatly benefited by following these teachings, and I have been inspired to share these with you through this book. As an immigrant myself, I empathise with the challenges faced by new immigrants. I have written this book to be a beacon of hope and possibility as you work your way to achieving the Canadian Dream.

CHAPTER 1
Arrival

Air Canada flight 2092 landed at Pearson International Airport in Mississauga at 2:00 pm EST. The passengers exited the plane and approached the concourse. One of the new immigrants is a 32-year-old Indian. While he exited the plane, his fingers grazed the surface of his bag pack. He touched the right side of his pocket to sense his cellphone and the left side to feel the bump of his wallet. He opened his passport to the Canada visa page, made sure he had his boarding pass, and said to himself, "I have everything."

This is the first time he is travelling to Canada. The 22-hour travel has made him tired and weary. His mind is filled with excitement, fear, confusion, and anticipation at the same time. He thought to himself, *I hope everything goes well. I hope I have everything I need!* As he descends down the escalator, he read a sign at the entrance: "Bienvenue au Canada" – "Welcome to Canada."

He was greeted by volunteers who asked him, "Are you a new immigrant?"

"Yes," he said, nodding his head.

"Welcome to Canada. Line up this way, please." He waited in line with other new immigrants from all over the world who came with a dream to the land of the maple leaf. Standing in line, his heart beat faster as he approached the immigration officer.

"Good Afternoon, sir," the immigration officer said, through the microphone on the other side of the glass.

"Good afternoon," he replied.

"May I see your passport and visa?"

With fear hovering his mind, he responded, "Here it izz… Off… Officer," and he handed over his passport with the boarding pass as a bookmark for the visa page.

"May I have your document?" the officer asked.

Perplexed, the man said, "Which document?"

"Do you plan to go back from where you came?" the officer questioned, with sarcasm. The Indian chap, seemingly lost, said, "Eh, which documents?"

"I need your landing papers," the officer replied.

"Oh! Yes, yes!" he said, with a sigh of relief. "I have my landing papers in the bag. I'll give you my landing papers, so please give me a second." He scrambled through his bag to grab a file. He pulled out the landing paper and handed it to the officer. The officer verified his details on the immigration document by questioning him to match the details he provided to Immigration Canada.

"At which address do you want your Permanent Resident card to be sent to, Jim?" the officer asked.

"Yes sir, my name is Jim. Here is the address." Jim opened a text message in his cellphone and showed the officer the address of his aunt's house.

The officer took notes and replied, "You will receive your PR Card at this address. I have signed your landing paper. Here is your copy. Never lose this document."

"I won't," Jim promised. With an adrenalin-induced shivering hand, he put the landing papers into his file and packed his passport. He again checked his right and left pockets to feel his mobile and wallet. Carrying his bag, he proceeded to border security. "Scan your passport on the machines and fill in the details as guided," a Canadian Border Security Agency (CBSA) officer announced. Though

Jim had travelled to Europe and the Middle East in the past, he had never seen such automated machines in his life. He scanned his passport and filled in the details, anxious that he had traditional milk sweets in his bag and gifts for family. He hoped this didn't get him pulled over by the CBSA officer.

The officer looked at his declaration, checked the passport, and said, "You may proceed to the baggage receiving area."

Exhaling deeply, Jim approached the carousel, saw that there were luggage carts and a huge billboard that read the CIBC sponsors your baggage cart. *Bank with CIBC!* He wondered, *What on earth do the airport authorities think? Why would they charge passengers for baggage carts? Such an unwelcoming gesture to have visitors shell out money for baggage carts. I don't know if I will ever bank with CIBC. Anyway, thank you CIBC for the free cart.*

He grabbed a cart. He waited at the carousel and looked at bags being spit out of the snaking machine. Anxious, and after waiting for some time, he saw his grey bag and pulled it over. After a while, his second bag came out, and he dragged it over the carousel and dropped it on the baggage cart. He took his bags and moved to Customs. *I have cash to declare; it's my first time in Canada.* He darted his eyes at the officer.

"This way, please." The officer directs him to Customs. He walked down the aisle and approached the customs officer.

"I am a new immigrant," Jim told him. "I want to declare my belongings."

"Show me your passport, visa, and declaration," the customs officer asked. Jim provided the declaration and got the documents stamped. "Alrighty, you are good to go."

"Thank you, officer." Jim exchanges smiles with him.

Sighing again with a sense of relief, he smiled. *Doing things the first time always make me anxious. I'm glad this went well. I have finally landed in Canada and completed the immigration process. I am now a Canadian PR Holder!*

He went out and walked along the arrival corridor to reach the information desk. His aunt had asked him to use the pay phone to call her for pick-up when he reached the airport.

He dropped in the coins, but the pay phone didn't respond. He was nervous again and looked around to see if he could find help.

He asked a man standing next to him, "Excuse me, can you please help me with the phone? I am unable to make a call."

The man looked at the pay phone and replied, "Forget this, use my cellphone and make your call."

Whoa! This guy is helpful. Seems that Canadians are very welcoming and helpful people. Receiving help from a stranger back home may not have been so swift. Jim made the call and waited for his aunt. His eyes moved to the red and brown kiosk named Tim Hortons. *Oh! This must be the coffee chain auntie was telling me about. This is my chance to grab a doughnut and coffee.* Jim stood in line.

"What would you like to have?" the barista asked.

"I'd like to have a double chocolate doughnut and a small coffee."

"How would you like to have the coffee?" she asked. The question baffled Jim. *Aren't coffees served with milk and sugar?* "May I have a regular coffee with milk... and sugar?" he answered.

"How much sugar would you like?"

"Two spoons," Jim answered.

"Sir, you seem to be new in Canada," she replied.

"Yes, I just arrived."

"Next time you order a coffee, don't ask for a regular coffee, ask for a double-double."

"What does a double-double mean?"

"The double-double coffee contains servings of 2 creams and 2 sugars. It's the most preferred coffee for most Canadians. If you ask for regular coffee, we'll serve you black coffee."

"Oh! Thanks for informing me." Jim picked up his order and took a seat. He sipped the coffee. *Aggh, this is bitter. Thankfully I got a doughnut. I think I'll need 4 creams and 4 sugars in my coffee the next time.* Eating his doughnut carefully, making sure there was enough doughnut to combine with each sip of bitter coffee, Jim waited for his aunt. *I may have travelled to many countries, but this country has its own unique ways of doing things.*

His aunt picked him from Terminal 1 and after greeting each other warmly, his aunt drove them to her home. In disbelief, he had finally received Permanent Residency in Canada. He thought back in time to the date he had applied for immigration. "Despite the fact that my application was returned the first time by CIC, I tried again and kept visualising this day vividly in my mind," he tells his aunt. "I am pinching myself in disbelief that I have finally landed here as a resident in Canada." *Thoughts mixed with emotional intensity have tremendous power to make things happen. I wonder if I can use this to create a fulfilling life for me and my family in Canada.*

Jim was married to a charming girl he met at work, and just six months before his trip. Everything was going as planned. He had a corporate job with a seven-figure income, a place to live, a car, and he was debt-free back in his home country. Life seemed to be on a roll for him. It seemed that he could have continued in the same company year after year and retired happily. Very reluctantly, he decided to immigrate to Canada. His wife was back in his home country living with his family until she could come.

The biggest worry on his mind was to sponsor his wife, Helen, at the earliest so they could live together in Canada. *I hope I get a well-paying job so I can sponsor her.*

CHAPTER 2

Rendezvous

Jimmy, nicknamed Jim by his family, started a modest life in Canada living in the basement of his Aunt Annie's house. His aunt was his source of moral support in the new country that he planned to make his homeland. Had his aunt and his mom not persuaded him, Jim would not have embarked on migrating to Canada. After arriving, Jim started applying for jobs that matched his profile. But he didn't receive any interview calls. Frustrated with the results, he complained about the job situation to his aunt. "Why am I not getting any interview calls? I've been applying for two months now."

Concerned by Jim's frustration, Aunt Annie talked to him. "Jim, Canada is a different country. Things here are done differently. What worked back home will not work here. You need to set a plan for yourself, decide a timeline. You need to start with obtaining your driver's licence, begin networking with people, apply for volunteering activities, and make yourself visible. Take up any job you get. It is not probable you will get a job of your liking sitting at home."

"Aunt Annie, I plan to visit the newcomer's employment centre in our area," Jim said. "That is what I have been prescribed to do by the Canadian Immigrant Integration Program (CIIP) facilitator. They will help me find suitable employment."

"Whatever you plan to do, ensure you are acting on it," she advised. His aunt knew time was of the essence for every new immigrant, and that if Jim didn't start earning soon, he would get into a negative-thinking downward spiral.

As directed by the CIIP facilitator, Jim decided to visit the employment services center in his area. The center was a five-minute drive; however, Jim took the bus. It took him 20 minutes to reach the center. *I was told that Canada is a developed country, but the transportation system is inefficient. It would have taken me 30 minutes to jog here while the bus takes 20 minutes. This is ridiculous!*

Nonetheless, he arrived at the employment center. "Hi, "I'm Jim," he said to the receptionist. "I'm a new immigrant and want to meet an employment facilitator."

"Welcome to Canada," the receptionist replied. "Please fill in your details on this form and return it to me."

While filling out the form, Jim read a requirement on it. CLB score: _______. Perplexed, Jim asked, "What does CLB stand for?"

"It's the Canadian Language Benchmark," she said. You need to provide your English language proficiency scores."

"But I have my IELTS scores. Won't the IELTS scores be accepted?" he asked her.

"You will have to take the CLB test and provide your scores here. You can take your first test for free at a nearby Center of Education and Training (CET)."

"Why do I need to take an English language test again when I have spent money to obtain IELTS test scores?"

"It is a requirement to process every application."

"Even after I have scored 8 bands? This is so frustrating."

"Sir," the receptionist tried to reassure him. "It is a short test and you will get the results immediately. Using the CLB scores we will be able to assist you with placement services. In the meanwhile, we'll assign you to an employment facilitator."

After completing the formalities, Jim was ushered to meet his facilitator.

"Hello Jim, I'm Karen. I will assist you with your settlement in Canada."

"It's nice to meet you, Karen" Jim greeted her back.

"What is it that I can help you with today?" she asked him.

"I am looking for a job," Jim stated.

"I see you have an MBA in finance. Currently, we have jobs for customer services, call center reps, security guards, and – "

"But, Karen," Jim interrupted her, "I am looking for a job that is related to what I have been doing back in my home country. I want to work with something related to my field."

"Is there any specific company you are looking for?" she asked.

"I'm not worried about the company," Jim answered. I am concerned about the work profile."

Karen took another glance at his intake form and replied, "If you have specific jobs that you have been pursuing, please let me know. I can contact the company to inquire regarding their position requirements. I will need your CLB scores before I can proceed."

"I will get you the CLB scores, Karen. I hope you can find me a job soon."

Karen nodded as she passed him a paper, "Please keep this, Jim. This is our monthly event calendar. You'll find the time and dates of the various trainings we provide immigrants."

Jim took the piece of paper and asked her, hesitatingly, "Are all these events free?"

"Yes," Karen replied. "They are funded by taxpayer's money."

"I hope," Jim responded with a nervous laugh. "I am funding your organisation soon."

"Of course!" she said. "We are here to enable you to be gainfully employed."

"I'll email you my CLB details, my resume, and the jobs I am interested in applying," Jim told her.

"Alrighty!" Karen replied, as she shook his hand. "All the best."

Jim took the CLB test where he scored 8 in all the parameters. Looking at the results, Jim thought, *I wonder why they need new immigrants like me to re-do an English language test like the CLB when its difficulty level is way below that of the IELTS? At least the first attempt is free. Such a waste of time and money of the government and new immigrants.*

Jim emailed his resume, the CLB test scores, and the job postings he was interested in to Karen. Karen reviewed his documents and gave him a call. "How are you, Jim?" she asked after he answered.

"I'm doing fine."

"I've had a look at the documents you sent me. You have scored well on your CLB test. However, I see that your resume isn't customised to the job posting you're interested in."

"What is a customised resume?" Jim asked, confused.

"Your resume is generic," she responded. "You need to tailor your experience to match the job requirements posted by the employer."

"No wonder I haven't been receiving any interview calls," Jim said.

"I would recommend you attend our training on resume writing and interview sessions," she offered. "This is a hands-on training session that will provide you with insight about the expectations of employers. It will teach you the how-to's for applying jobs here in Canada."

"Ok, thanks, Karen. I'll attend the next sessions."

Jim looked up the training calendar Karen provided him and signed up to attend the next available training session. When he got there, he found the room filled with people from diverse fields, ethnicity, and experience. Karen started teaching the audience the ropes of a job application in Canada.

"You may have all the experience in the world, but when you are applying for a position, you need to ensure that your resume matches the job application," Karen told them. "The employer is only interested in what you can do for them and their needs, so serve them accordingly. Scrap the rest of your experience. You don't need to show them everything you have done."

"Does this mean I have to re-write the resume each time I apply for a new job?" Jim asked.

"Yes," Karen said. "It's too much information for the employers. This is the way the system works in North America. Another important thing: ensure your English and grammar are crisp on your cover letter and resume. An error on either will get you rejected. You are competing with 200 to 300 applicants."

"How many applicants do you think the employer will select?" Jim asked.

"Ten?" "Six?" "Three?" The crowd shouted out.

"The employer will only select 3-5 applicants," she answered. "They don't have the time or patience to interview more candidates. You need to target being in the top 5 applicants. Once you get a seat at the table, you have a higher chance of landing the job. The hardest part of the job application process is to get yourself an interview. Research the company you are applying for. Treat them as you would treat a partner you are dating. You need to learn everything possible you could know about their needs and your role in their world."

Learning from the training, Jim thought, *interesting! I wish I had known this before.*

During the coffee break, Jim started interacting with the other participants. He was thoroughly impressed with the questions, comments, and discussions, and one in particular shared by a woman named Jessica. Jim walked up to Jessica and introduced himself.

"I was impressed by your comments during the discussion that ensued during the resume writing session," Jim said graciously.

"Oh, thank you," she replied. "By the way, it's pronounced as reh-zu-may and not ri-zum." Jim was taken aback and didn't know how to respond. "Employers will make interpretations of your persona from your pronunciations. So, it's wise to learn the correct pronunciations."

"Thanks for letting me know, Jessica," Jim answered. "Coming back to something you shared during the session, could you tell me more about technical talent being less valued than soft skills?"

"Technical talent is required but is underrated as compared to soft skills here in Canada."

"Why do you think so?" Jim asked her.

"I was born and brought up here in Canada," she answered. "My parents migrated to Canada from Jamaica. I studied fashion design and have been working as a sales rep in retail. It's challenging to repay my student loans, my rent, and groceries. In spite of years of study and hard work, I have not been able to get a break into the fashion industry. I earn minimum wage and lost my job recently due to downsizing."

"Is this the same challenge everyone faces in Canada?" Jim asked.

"I guess everybody does, Jim. I have friends and family as well who have had similar experiences."

Jim realised that breaking into the job market was not reserved as a challenge for new immigrants. Everyone faced the same hurdles in Canada.

"So, what do you plan to do next?" Jim was curious about her options.

"I'm here for this session to sharpen my job-hunting skills. If this doesn't help, I plan to take up another program with Sheridan college that offers a co-op program. I have seen higher success rates of getting placed when the institution offers a co-op program."

"What is a co-op program?" Jim asked her, curious.

"A co-op program allows a student to get hands-on work experience with an employer while they study. This is one way that gives job seekers the opportunity to obtain industry experience and helps develop contacts and references within the industry."

"Hmm," Jim pondered. "Why would you spend extra money when you already have a student loan?"

"This is my only hope," she said, shrugging. "In Canada, you've got to do what you got to do."

After the break, the participants assembled back in the training. Karen explained the importance of keyword searches and how recruiters employ software that screens resumes for keywords.

"One more thing, folks," Karen said to the group. "For your resume, you need to make sure you have keywords identified and addressed in your resume. Most employers have automated systems that screen resumes before they land in the hands of the recruiter. These automated systems screen documents with pre-determined keywords. So, you need to ensure you have the keywords weaved into your resume. Writing a resume is a piece of art that involves science. Your resume should act like a trojan's horse to bypass the automated screens. Some people use the header and footer to type in keywords and make the font white so they're not readable. Smart! But you should be careful. Most recruiters know this trick and if you get caught, you could lose your chance of getting a call for an interview. The interview process is equally important; go well prepared. Develop a portfolio."

"What is a portfolio?" another participant, Majid, asked.

"A portfolio is a binder that contains an index and tabs that provide work samples, certificates, awards, achievements, and references. All well crafted and organised to market yourself during the interview. Best practice is to visit the interview location a day before the interview and familiarise yourself with the location, the route to get there, and the average travel time. Visiting the interview location in advance gives you confidence and you will be better prepared to arrive on time. Many of you may be using public transit. Ensure you know whether the buses, trams, or trains are running on time. A tip for all of you – if you are running late due to public transit, spend the extra dollars and hire an Uber or Lyft. It's better than not reaching there in time."

Karen continued giving tips to the participants. "Ensure you are courteous to everyone on the way to the interview. The reason I'm telling you to be courteous to everyone is because I know of a candidate who applied for his dream job. On the way to the interview, he verbally abused a lady in another car, cut her off, and was rude. When he went to the interview location, he realised that the lady he misbehaved with was the manager he was interviewing with. She came to him and said, 'It was nice to meet you' and left. The interview never happened. He lost an opportunity of a lifetime. One more important thing is to collect contact cards of your interviewers and send each of them a personalised thank you message after the interview. Interviewers are sensitive to people who show interest and who follow up. If you don't hear back from them, then make sure you follow up after a specified time interval. I've seen candidates being called back for interviews after 6–8 months just because they followed up. When you follow up with the company, it shows your genuine interest in working for them and they may prefer you over another candidate."

Excited from the learning session, Jim went home fired up and started developing customised resumes for the positions he was interested in. He sent out multiple applications without success and set up a follow-up meeting with Karen.

"I customised my resume as per the information you gave me," he told Karen, "and have applied to 20 different companies. I've not heard back from any of them."

"This is not uncommon, Jim. Most new immigrants face similar challenges because they don't have Canadian work experience."

Frustrated by the conversation, Jim said, "Excuse my words, but this is a dumb system. Employers are unable to hire new immigrants because they don't have Canadian work experience? This is insane."

"It is hard to digest," she admitted, "but that is the reality. One needs to have good references to get their foot in the door."

"How does one expect a new immigrant to have good references, Karen?"

"Some people start at the bottom and work their way up the ladder. Others volunteer to get references. I'll share something with you which I don't share with most of my clients."

"Thanks Karen, but why would you share it selectively with me?"

"You ask too many questions, Jim," she said, honestly. "You have good English, you seem to be a genuine person with a nice personality. Most immigrants are not like you."

"Why would you generalise other immigrants?" Jim asked, somewhat offended.

"I know a few clients who fake their IELTS test scores, even their degrees," she responded. "Over the years, the government has realised this and have initiated the need to provide educational credential evaluations (ECE) completed. We have now come to learn that some immigrants have even faked their degrees with ECE reviewing agencies. That is the reason why employers are slow to hire new immigrants. It's hard to sift through so many new immigrants to find the right fit. It is unfortunate that many good immigrants like you get victimised because of the faults of a few. Coming back to the point, the Provincial scheme has an assistance program that new immigrants can avail. I need to inquire with the employers you're interested in whether they are interested in participating."

"Participating in what?" Jim asked.

"The government pays part of your salary and the employer pays the rest," she said. "This gives employers an incentive to hire new immigrants."

"Can you please help me with this, Karen?" he asked.

"I would love to," she replied, "but at the moment we have exhausted our funds for this year and are waiting for the new government to allocate more funds to extend this help to new immigrants."

"I wish I knew this before," Jim said, sadly. "I would have tried to monetize it when it was available."

Jim returned home feeling he had lost hope in the process of settling as a new immigrant, and frustrated with the kind of service provided to him by the settlement agency. *I can't get an interview call. I wonder how on earth will I ever be able to integrate into this country and make a decent living. I am paying rent to my aunt and my funds are depleting.*

Feeling low, Jim decided to soak up the sun. He walked out of his aunt's basement and began walking down the street. Staring at the sidewalk, he thought, *Did I make the right decision by coming to Canada? I shouldn't have come here in the first place. Back in my home country, life was good. I had everything. Life is hard here, and this country sucks. They asked for all my qualifications, my experience, my IELTS scores, I spent a fortune on the immigration process, and as soon as I land here, everything is null and void. Over and above, now they ask for Canadian work experience to get a job. How can I get a job without having lived and worked in Canada? It's like the chicken and the egg situation. Am I the chicken or the egg?*

CHAPTER 3
Frustration

Jim walked to the nearby park and saw a few people seated on the benches by the kid's splash pad. The kids were fully present and enjoying life while he was upset and feeling depressed. He found an empty bench and sat with his face down staring at the ground, contemplating how good his life was back in his home country. He missed his wife and family. A hand touched his shoulder and he looked up to see a middle-aged well-dressed man staring at him.

"Hello," the man said. "Are you new to the country?" Jim nodded his head yes.

"Welcome to Canada!" he said, joyfully.

What welcome? Is this the way the country treats new immigrants? he thought but politely said, "Thank you, sir," to the man standing before him who appeared to be from an Eastern European country by his accent. "I'm Jim."

"Call me Dave," he said, while sitting down on the bench beside Jim. "I see you're lost in thought."

Though reluctant to talk to anyone, Jim resisted his urge to be alone and responded, "Yes."

"Is there something on your mind that you wish to share with a stranger?" Dave asked.

"I'm looking for a job, not just any job. I want a job that pays well and is similar to what I was doing back in my country."

"Why do you want to do a job?" Dave asked.

Perplexed by the question, Jim said, "Of course I need a job, because I need to survive and pay my bills."

"Hmm," Dave answered, sensing Jim's frustration. "So what is stopping you from doing that?"

"I have applied to over 75 job positions in the past two months," Jim answered, in a slightly hostile voice, "but have not received a single interview call. My patience is running out."

"I understand," Dave said. "What do you want to do about it?"

"I don't know," Jim responded, glumly. "I'm even wondering if I made the right decision to come here in the first place. This place is so indifferent to new immigrants. The government asks for so many qualifications and requirements: IELTS scores, professional work experience as per the job categories for experienced professionals, Education Credential Evaluation, finances. But the day an immigrant lands here everything is invalid. I went to the career center and they asked me to complete a Canadian Language Benchmark (CLB) test to be eligible for help. Even if they are offering the test for free, why would they ask me to do that? I have already submitted my IELTS scores before I came here. The job postings they offer me are either labour jobs, security, trucking, and customer service. Even the security and trucking jobs need a licence. Forget that. All the jobs that are related to my profession also need a driving licence, a car, and insurance. One of the employment counselors mentioned that I'll need to re-educate myself to be employable. I have already provided my education credential evaluation to prove I am employable and provided my job references including relevant experience to the government already. The entire immigration system in this country is rigged. All the government wants is for new immigrants to come here and spend their hard-earned money to obtain an education without the guarantee to get a job."

Dave patiently listened to Jim and smiled. "Why are you smiling?" Jim asked. "My wife is in my home country, and I need to have a job to sponsor her Permanent Residence. The more I delay, the more time it will take to get her here."

Dave laid his hand on Jim's shoulder. "Why did you come here, Jim?"

Jim sat up with the shift of the conversation. "To have a better life."

"That's it?" Dave prodded. "I mean, what is it that that you didn't have in your home country that brought you here?"

"I came here to make more money," Jim responded.

"What stopped you from making more money back in your home country?" Dave asked. "The dollar-to-local currency conversion helps accumulate money. So when you get the money, would you go back?"

"No," Jim stated, emphatically.

"So what brings you here?" Dave persisted.

"There is lot of corruption," Jim answered. "Politics, there is no value for life, and the pollution is getting from bad to worse every day."

"Are you suggesting that you want to go back to that same country where you came from?" Dave asked.

"Maybe, yes", Jim said, completely confused at this point, feeling trapped by Dave's questions.

"You aren't clear in your mind what you really want, are you?" Dave commented.

"I am clear," Jim retorted. "I want a good job here in Canada, a job that pays good money so that I can settle down here with my wife."

"What if what you wish for doesn't happen?" Dave asked.

Jim looked down, shrugged his shoulders, confused again. "I wish I hadn't come here in the first place," he grumbled.

"You can't change the past," Dave replied.

"Life was so easy back in my home country," Jim said. "Life is so hard here in Canada."

"What makes life difficult here in Canada, Jim?"

"The way things are set up here, Dave. The employers are cynical for hiring new immigrants. The government doesn't seem to care or do anything concrete to make life easier for new immigrants. The necessity to have a driver's licence and a car, the need to go back to school again, the need to start from scratch. Last but not the least, the taxes. Working at minimum wage and one still pays so much in taxes. The other day a friend of my aunt mentioned that her mother-in-law had to wait for eight months in pain to get a date for her knee surgery."

Dave smiled, listening intently. "What about you, Jim? You never mentioned yourself in this long list of yours."

"Why me, I think," Jim responded. "I'm not responsible for the way things are set up here. What have I to do with it?"

"Are you the only immigrant coming to this country who feels this way?" Dave inquired. "Do you think everyone who came to this country had an unfair advantage at the outset?"

"I don't know," Jim replied. "I think most people who come to this country face the same challenges I am facing."

"Do you think they were any different from you?" Dave asked.

"No!" Jim replied fiercely.

"Did they settle here and make a life for themselves?" Dave asked.

"Looking at the growing community, I would say yes to that," Jim replied.

"Do you think they would have managed to settle here had they regretted coming here?" Dave persisted with his questioning.

"No," Jim responded, "but they came here a long time ago. Things were easier back then. Things are much harder nowadays."

"Says who?" Dave asked, with a grin.

"Look at the job market," Jim said, waving his hand around. "It is so slow. All the jobs available are survival jobs. I have an MBA in finance. I came here not to sweep floors and clean toilets, drive a truck or do a security job. I would rather get employed in a good company, get paid well, and I would be happy to pay my share of higher taxes. Look at what the government policies and employers have done! They attract the cream-of-the-crop population from other countries, bring them here, and then make them minimum wage workers! Even the freaking government is losing tax money by not opening avenues for highly skilled immigrants like myself. If they would build a system where new immigrants get jobs equivalent to their abilities, they would start being the government's cash machine rather than working on minimum wage flipping burgers or serving coffee."

Dave interrupted Jim's thoughts by putting his hand up. "Does cursing the existing system help you get a better paying job?"

"I hope," Jim answered. "If I could get a job cursing the system, I would do it more often."

Knowing that Jim was on a rant, Dave said sternly, "Possibly that's why you are without a job. Don't try to change the system, Jim. This system has been there even before you came here. The government knows the chokeholds and is working to improve the integration process. I can tell you this, things were much more difficult back in the day when I came here as a new immigrant, just like you, young in my mid-twenties. I learned this over the years and I'm sharing this with you. Don't curse what you have; most people yearn to have what you already have. Ask yourself this question: How many people do you know in your home country who would have fought tooth and nail to come here to Canada and would be willing to do anything that you mentioned that you don't want to do?"

Jim thought and said, "Most people don't know what they are getting into when they plan to come here. It's only after they come here that they realise what they've bought into."

"Then go back!" Dave said firmly. "Why are you staying here when you are not happy? Happy is where the heart is, and never do anything that doesn't make you happy. Tell me this: what would you do if you went back to your country?"

"I would look for a job in my previous company or hunt for another job," Jim answered quickly.

"What if you got the job in your home country," Dave asked. "Would you be happy?"

"Umm, yes," Jim replied. "I would be happy if I got the job."

"Then what?" Dave said, not backing down. "You said you weren't happy and came here because of the corruption, politics, and pollution. You would go back to the same place? Wouldn't you regret that you had the opportunity to come and settle in this first world country and make a life for yourself and for generations to come?"

"Yes," Jim replied.

"I would," Dave answered. "I have seen many people and families who started their lust for the west, came here, went back, came back again, and went back. Many of them changed countries with some going to Australia, the U.S., and were not happy there either. It's not about the country that you are in. It's about you and what you do with what is provided to you. Every country has its own benefits and limitations. And each country is working to make life better for its people every day, or at least they try to. But until the people of the nation do not realise their role in their own personal growth, they will never be happy wherever they go. Happiness lies within, not without; opportunities lie within, not without; abundance lies within, not without. It all lies within."

Dave got up. "It's getting dark and my wife must be waiting for me. Let's meet again, Jim."

"Same place?" Jim asked.

"No, at my house," Dave responded. "I'll introduce you to my wife, Emilia, and our son."

"What's your address?" Jim asked.

"3267 Hillcroft Drive," Dave said. "But, before we meet again, I want you to go back and make up your mind whether you want to stay here or return back."

CHAPTER 4
Mentoring

Jim walked toward the park. Dave's house was nearby.

"You're still in Canada, I see," Dave said as Jim approached his home. "What do you prefer, tea or coffee?"

"I'll have tea," Jim responded as he clasped Dave's hand in greeting.

Dave introduced Jim to his wife Emilia and their son Adrian, then Emilia left for the kitchen to make tea. "The reason I called you over to my place is to share my story and challenges as a new immigrant," Dave stated, as they sat down in his living room. "Perhaps it will inspire you to make a decision about Canada. When I migrated to Canada with my wife, there was a drastic change in the way we lived our lives. Things were not easy in the initial years. I experienced some of the same challenges that you are facing now. I avoided working survival jobs in the hopes that I would get a job at par with what I was qualified for. I realised over the years of living in this country that I had to prepare myself and my family for immigration to Canada. It's similar to preparing myself when I had to change jobs, move into a new house, purchase a new car, and welcome a new child in the family. Everything I received in life tested me for my worthiness. My wife tested me before she said yes to my proposal."

Dave's wife overheard their conversation as she walked into the living room with the tea tray. The three of them shared some light banter about the tests they put their spouses through before marriage while Emilia set the tea tray down on the coffee table. "I'd love to stay and talk more," Emilia said. "Another day perhaps, but think I'll just leave you two alone to catch up," she said and left the room.

"One thing I didn't do while I was settling in Canada was to take pictures," Dave said while turning his attention back to Jim and filling their teacups. "I recommend taking pictures about your journey as a new immigrant in Canada. It's a good tool to share your success story some years down the line with other immigrants. When times get tough and your prayers seem to never come true, open these pictures and look at the progress you've made. The past will inspire you to take action and build a prosperous future in Canada. This country tests an immigrant's determination to live here. You need to prepare and be ready mentally, spiritually, and physically to receive the gifts of life. You need to prepare and grow your skillset, your mindset, and resilience."

"I enjoy you sharing your experiences with me and telling me to develop myself," Jim replied thoughtfully while stirring sugar into his tea. "All of this is ok, but how do I build these qualities in me?"

"I was helped by many people to overcome some of the challenges when I was a new immigrant in Canada," Dave answered, "and so I want to pay it forward by helping you settle in this country."

"I'm so grateful," Jim said, humbly.

Dave abruptly turned the conversation. "Have you been to a funeral lately?"

"No, but I've attended them before," Jim replied. "Why are you asking me?"

"What was the predominant thought process while at the funeral?"

"I guess that death can come at any time."

"How did the experience make you feel?"

Jim stared at the floor. "I felt very uncertain. That anything can happen to me anytime. I may not have as much time as I think I have."

"What does it mean to you, Jim?"

"I felt I should live my life preciously."

Inquisitively, Dave asked, "Preciously?"

"I should live my life to the fullest. I should complete the important things I plan to because there may not be more time. We live life thinking we have a lot of time unaware that life keeps passing by and that the end can happen any moment."

"I find your thoughts intriguing, Jim," Dave said. "I used the death analogy when I felt low and lonely. It helped me re-focus on my goal when life's challenges felt too overwhelming."

"That's counterintuitive, Dave. Some people contemplate committing suicide when they're troubled by life."

"It's how you look at it, Jim. I used death as a reminder of the limited time we have. And that my current troubles won't last long as life keeps changing. Some others look at death as an escape from their troubles and think their troubles will never end. I used to ask myself, 'What I would be doing if today was my last day?'"

"If today was my last day," Jim retorted, "I would rather spend it with my family than living it here alone in Canada away from my family."

"That's why you're in Canada, to build a life for your family," Dave said. "Use death as a reminder of a limited life - not an escape plan. While contemplating on death, don't lose focus on the long-term goal you are working towards for your family."

"I'm not convinced with what you're saying, Dave."

"I don't want to convince you, Jim. I'm sharing what worked for me. It may or may not work for you. You have to decide for yourself."

Dave poured some more tea into their cups. "Sooo, let's shift some gears and look at your homework. Did you make up your mind whether to stay or leave Canada?"

"You know, Dave," Jim started, "the more I think about it, the more confused I get. My mind is acting like a monkey on hot bricks. It has been so difficult to make a decision. I keep drifting, thinking how good things were back in my home country, and whether things will be better in the future or will I live my life like a nobody here."

"You get to decide!" Dave exclaimed. "That's the advantage of being human. You can be whatever you want. But you need to know why."

Jim's eyebrows raised. "Why?" he asked.

"Why is a powerful word, Jim, and it has changed the world. It caused man to land on the moon, the development of the iPhone, and the space race to Mars. Without a *why* nothing can be achieved. What is your why, Jim? Why do you want to settle in Canada? And don't tell me it's because you want a better life."

"I don't know my why, Dave," Jim responded. "If I know my why, would it change my attitude?"

"Everything!" Dave exclaimed. "It will change everything once you know your why."

"Can you guide me to find my why?" Jim asked him.

"Yes, I can. I'll help you find your why, but I need you to promise me that you will commit yourself to instill a positive mindset for looking at life as a new immigrant in Canada. Work on your dreams of settling in this country."

A little hesitantly, Jim said, "I will."

"Do I have your commitment?" Dave asked, earnestly.

"Yeah," Jim answered, "I'm not confident, but I want to do this."

"Thanks for your honesty, Jim," Dave said. "Tell me a few things that caused you the most pain while you were in your home country. Something that you hate to your core, and there is nothing in the world that can change it for you."

After thinking for a while, Jim replied, "There are many."

"Think of any one thing. It has to be from the list of things you mentioned to me last time we met. What is the one thing that disgusts you the most about your country?"

Jim scanned through his thoughts. "The air pollution. If the pollution didn't exist, I would go back to my home country."

"Do you think the pollution is going to go away in the next 5-10 years in your home country?" With a sad look on his face, Jim replied, "No Dave. The air-pollution problem is not going to be solved in the next decade. In fact, things are getting worse. The Bill and Melinda Gates Foundation conducted a research study that determined the country's toxic air claimed 12.4 million lives in 2017 alone."

Jim continued. "Statistically, this figure accounts for 12.5% as the cause of deaths recorded in the year. I have come to realise that there is a genre of people who are leaving the country or relocating to less polluted cities within the country. Media calls them the 'pollution immigrants'. I believe I am one of them."

"Interesting! Do you see what you have done, Jim?"

"There's more, Dave," Jim said, glumly. "Each year a growing number of smart, wealthy people are migrating from the country to protect the health of their kids, their parents, and themselves. The government back home is focussing on development alone, with not much being done to curb pollution in general, and air pollution in particular."

"You have taken the right decision to move here considering the long-term benefits for you and your family," Dave said, decisively. "Imagine what would life be if you would continue staying in the country where the air pollution is deteriorating each day."

"It's nothing less than a gas chamber," Jim added, "where people don't realise they are dying because they don't see the immediate effects on their health."

"It is synonymous to the proverbial story of the frog," Dave said. "If you throw a frog into a pail of boiling water, it will immediately jump out. But if you put the frog into a pail and slowly heat the water, the frog, unsuspecting, will slowly be cooked to death."

Jim agreed, thinking about how members of his family became sick often because of the air quality in his home country.

"But let's go back to your answer," Dave continued. "Every time you feel like giving up on yourself, think about the consequences. Look up the articles and research information online that provides details about how bad things are. If this doesn't help, see videos on the level of pollution in your home country and resulting deterioration of health effects. Create a sense of dissatisfaction in your mind by inflicting pain to the thought of going back. Think about all the negative things that may have happened to you in the past, happening in the present, and that will continue to happen to you and your family in the future if you go back. The pain of going back should be much more than the pain you experience of not getting a job of your liking. Think in your mind about the benefits of staying. Think about all the good things that Canada has to offer, free clean air, free education, freedom of speech, human rights, a better standard of living, free health care."

"But not everything here is perfect, Dave," Jim said. "You will never find perfect, neither in yourself or externally."

"Search for reasons, not perfection, Jim. You need enough reasons to be able to direct yourself to do the things you need to do to settle in Canada."

"I'll remember that," Jim told him. "Thanks for the tea talk, but I think I should get going."

"Go prepare a list of goals you want to accomplish," Dave said. "For the next 3 months, one year, three years, and five years."

"Come on Dave, please don't get started with goal setting," Jim pleaded. "I have done it before. It doesn't help!"

"Really?" Dave said, a bit sarcastically. "Why do you think it doesn't help?"

Jim threw his hands up in disgust. "This is all pumped up self-help concepts that don't work in the real world."

"Never mind that," Dave said. "For now, just go and try to set these goals."

"Ok, Dave," Jim said reluctantly, "only because you're asking me."

"Great," Dave said. "Let's meet again when you complete your list."

CHAPTER 5
Mindset

Jim visited Dave's house again after a few weeks. "Morning, Dave," Jim said happily, as Dave stepped aside to let him enter.

"How are you doing?" Dave asked.

"I'm getting better," Jim replied.

"I like the sound of your answer," Dave said. "It sounds optimistic."

"I see a new car in your driveway," Jim said.

"Yes, I leased it," Dave replied, "to write off some of my taxes."

"How do you manage to do that kind of sorcery?" Jim said.

"That's another topic for another day," Dave said, laughing. "Let's get back to where we left last time we met."

"Take a look at my list," Jim said, handing him some papers. Dave took the papers to read and they both sat down in the living room.

First 3 months:

1. Get a job like I had while I was working back home.
2. A job that pays at least $50,000 per year.
3. Submit my wife's sponsorship application.
4. Visit my wife for our wedding anniversary this
   year.

First 1 Year:

1. Get a job paying $ 80,000 annually.
2. Rent an apartment to live with my wife.
3. Save and invest money to make a down-payment for a house.

3 Years:

1. Get a mortgage and buy my own house here in Canada.
2. Invite my family for a visit to Canada.
3. Invest and make a recurring income on my invested money.

5 Years:

1. Pay-off my mortgage on the house.
2. Earn so much money that I can do more of the things I enjoy rather than working.
3. Make a trip to my home country whenever I want.

"I'm glad you did your homework," Dave said, looking up from Jim's work, "but you didn't mention the things that you will commit to in order to able to achieve these goals."

"Why do I need to do that, Dave?"

"How are you going to achieve your goals unless you have a clear and concise plan of action to achieve it?" Create a table, write your goals to the far left, and write critical things that you need to do on the right side in order to achieve these goals."

"Here," Dave said, handing him a pencil sitting on the table. "Start scribbling."

Jim prepared the plan to achieve his goals on the back side of the papers.

Goals	Actions
1. Get a comparable job that pays $50,000 per year	• Study the Canadian job market • Network with industry professionals • Craft a professional resume and cover Letter • Apply for relevant positions
2. Submit my Wife's sponsorship application	• Download the Sponsorship application forms • Seek help from a friend or settlement services to complete the application
3. Visit my wife for our wedding anniversary	• Earn money for the flight tickets • Book the flight tickets
4. Get a better job paying $80,000 per year	• Identify professional qualifications that will help me improve my market value • Enroll and complete the professional qualification • Apply for jobs that pay a higher salary
5. Rent an apartment to live with my wife	• Identify an area where you are comfortable to live • Look for homes on Kijiji advertising, and rent the place
6. Save and invest money to make a	• Save money for down-payment of a house

Goals	Actions
down-payment for a house	• Keep a monthly log of spending • Identify and trim unwanted expenses such as coffee, eating out, cinema
7. Get a mortgage and buy my own house here in Canada	• Identify a good realtor • Search for houses in a good location • Obtain a bank loan and bid for a house • Purchase the house
8. Invite family to Canada	• Save money for their travel • Apply for their visa and flight tickets
9. Invest and make a recurring income on invested money	• Study the stock market • Save money to invest • Open a Questrade trading account and invest money in ETFs • Max out the TFSA and RRSP limits
10. Pay-off my mortgage on the house	• Save and grow approximately $400,000 to pay-off the mortgage
11. Earn so much money that I can do more of the things I enjoy, than working	• Identify business ideas to earn additional income • Work on this idea and grow it to multiply my income
12. Make a trip to home country whenever I want	• Make sufficient money to fly to my home country whenever I want • Develop a system that will help me delegate my work when I am away

"This is a good start, Jim," Dave said, after looking it over. "What did you notice while developing this?"

"I find that most of my goals are over ambitious," Jim said. "There will be much more preparation needed, and more time to achieve these goals. Writing down your goals with the needed actions will help you make realistic assumptions of time and effort to achieve them."

"My advice to you is this," Dave said. "While writing down your goals, review them and test them with a plan of action to back them up. Writing a plan of action is the key to beta test your goals and verify whether they are achievable. Now that you have your goals ready, keep them aside and review them at regular intervals. You will find that divine forces are set in motion to help you attain your goals."

"Are you telling me about Rhonda Byrne's book, *The Secret?*" Jim asked.

"No, Jim. I'm sharing the facts that have worked for me. If you want to grow, you need to have two things – a mindset that enables you to focus on your goals and the action you will take to do things that are necessary to achieve them. When the power of intent and the power of fruitful labour amalgamate, marvellous things are achieved. What will you do if you're unable to get a job of your liking in the first three months?"

"I don't know," Jim answered. "Can you get me a job, Dave?"

"I would love to help you," Dave said, "but if I help you, you won't grow. You must learn to earn your keep."

This was not the reply Jim was expecting. Dave looked at him squarely. "I cannot give you a job, but I can give you the tools to get the job or create one for yourself and others."

Jim smiled in a disgruntled manner, nodding his head. "I need a job, and I need it right now."

"Common people believe that if they lose something great, they may not be able to recover it," Dave said. "An achiever like you gives up something great to gain something greater."

"What do you see in me that I don't see in myself?" Jim asked him.

"You are a risk taker," Dave responded. "You left a secure job and your family and friends to come and settle here in Canada. This itself proves that you are more than you think you are. It's just that you need to trust yourself, be patient, and do the things that will lead you to be able to settle in this country."

"Life is tough," Jim replied. "How can I make good money with so many odds shored up against me?"

"If you want to make a lot of money, you must solve a bigger problem, Dave answered. "Right now, your problems are small. To some other people, it isn't even a problem. It's how you look at it. Imagine this," Dave explained, "if Elon Musk was in your situation. What do you think he would do?"

"Who is Elon Musk?" Jim asked, confused.

"Musk is an entrepreneur and leads Tesla – the electric car company and SpaceX," Dave said.

"Oh," Jim said. "I remember, he started a company because he didn't get hired. I don't have skills like Elon Musk, Dave. Neither do I have the passion to start a business at this point. All I want is to be able to get a good job that pays my bills."

"Identify your uniqueness that you bring to this country, Jim. Start with what you have and do what you can," Dave advised.

"I have tried time and again for so many jobs that I am an expert at," Jim said. "I don't receive any interview calls. Every job fair around the city is hiring for bottom of the pyramid positions: warehouse workers, security guards, customer service representatives, truck drivers - you name it. I didn't come to this country to do menial labour jobs. I came here to have a good future, to work with dignity, and have a happy life for my family."

"Learn a new skill and make yourself rich," Dave responded. "Start in a warehouse and work your way up, if you will."

"I don't want to work at a warehouse or any of those low-paying jobs, Dave."

"I suggest you have control on your cash flow then, Jim. It's the oxygen for an individual, a family, and any organisation. I understand you may have brought money that you saved for yourself."

"Yes," Jim said.

"It will deplete unless you work and replenish your treasury," Dave said. "The first few months of an immigrant's life are very crucial. It's a good indicator whether an immigrant determines to stay or leave."

"Now you are scaring me," Jim said. "As I mention time and again, I am looking for a place where I can get a job related to my field."

"I know of a place that can help you do that," Dave offered, "but you won't get the job outright."

"What do I need to do then, Dave?"

"You must go to this adult education school named Saint Gabriel, Dave answered. "It's in Malton, Mississauga. They have programs that help new immigrants understand what the Canadian employers need and they will train you to refurbish your resume. They teach you how to match your skills with the demand in the industry. Once you complete the program, there will be a high probability that you may get a job similar to the work you did in your home country, or a job that leverages your skills for the employer."

"What do I have to do?" Jim said, curiously.

"When you enroll in their program, you need to provide them with a CLB score and a small dollar deposit to ensure you are committed to the program, Dave answered. "They will train you for seven weeks and help you get a volunteer position in a field of your liking with an organisation. This training is followed by 14 weeks of on-the-job volunteering."

"That is a long time to work for free," Jim said, somewhat deflated. "Do they guarantee a job at the end of the work period?"

"Well, Jim, nothing is guaranteed in life; not even life itself. When you go there and volunteer, you are increasing your probability of getting a job. Considering your current situation, this is the best advice I can offer."

"How long are the classes and the volunteer workdays?" Jim asked.

"They are full days," Dave answered. "It's like the routine eight-hour workday."

Jim felt his stomach churn. "Full days for over three months. How will I survive?"

"I have known people who work part-time to pay their bills and attend the program," Dave answered. "Many of them have been now gainfully employed since they completed the program. The choice is yours. Struggle your butt off for these initial months and have a higher probability of getting a job or keep hoping that someone will come by and give you a job. I personally believe you have a higher chance of getting a job if you take my advice."

"What happens after the volunteer work is over?" Jim asked.

"Well," Dave started, "if the organisation where you work needs a person for the position you volunteer for, you may get the job or else you will get a good reference that may help you get a job you are looking for. This is how you create Canadian work experience by volunteering for an organisation that is looking for people like you, prove yourself, and get hired. Create more value than you get paid for."

"What do you mean?" Jim asked, not believing his ears. "I will be working for free anyway!"

"What I am trying to convey, Jim, is to determine how much would they pay you if you were working for them as a regular employee. Then work to deliver more value than the paycheck you would receive. When you do this, you become a desirable employee and when a position comes, they won't resist hiring you."

"Why do you think people working for $13 an hour?" Dave continued. "They're not as valuable to the business. Not only that, the owner of the business can replace them and get a new person to do the job in an instant. You also don't want to be doing a wage-earning job for too long."

"Why?" Jim asked.

"Technology!" Dave answered. "It's the new competition, the thing that is replacing jobs that don't create much value. Like the self check-out machines at

Walmart and other superstores. They're using the customer's time and effort to get the job done. These machines will eventually replace the cashiers. Amazon Go is a step ahead and has installed smart shopping technology that enables you to go into the store, pick what you need and walk out without passing the checkout With such disruptive technology that pushes the envelope, it's not far off when most stores will have this as standard systems. It makes life easier, cheaper, and efficient for the business owner but creates job losses. So don't hang around in a job that can be replaced by technology in the long run. You should only use it as a means to get to where you need to go."

"But, Dave, I have an MBA!"

"Jim," Dave said, shaking his head. "Understand this: you need to do what you hate to do in order to get to where you want to be. Your ability to do the things that you may hate will give you the possibility to achieve the things you have never had.

"I can't imagine myself doing something small," Jim said, shaking his head. "We were taught as kids, study well or you'll have to do menial jobs to survive. I did not study so much to do menial jobs."

"Suck up your ego," Dave told Jim. "It's social conditioning that is hindering you. Shed useless skin to uncover the new you. There is much to lose and nothing to gain by clinging on to old value systems. If you want to belong to a group of successful immigrants, you need to pay a membership fee. Now go and look for a job that gets the cash flowing for you. Meet me next week and we'll see how things are working out for you."

Jim left feeling dejected but followed Dave's recommendation and started applying for warehouse jobs. To his surprise, Jim got an interview call within a few hours. The recruiter arranged an interview the very next day. *At least I'll be able to use Canadian money to pay Canadian bills. The savings I brought from home will be reserved.*

Jim prepared for his interview in formal clothes: a shirt, tie, and formal pants. At the interview, he saw most of the applicants were dressed down in casual clothes, jeans, and sweatshirts. All of the applicants were asked to fill in application forms and wait their turn. The interviewers introduced themselves and mentioned that they started their career at the bottom and climbed the ladder to become production leads and human resource personnel.

The interview proved to be very basic and he got shortlisted for the second round. The interview panel invited the shortlisted candidates into a conference room. Cue cards were laid out for each candidate to speak on the given topic. Jim thought, *so much drama for a labour position!*

Jim met a Punjabi couple at the interview who had arrived just a week ago. They were excited to get their first job. Jim was amused by their enthusiasm. While waiting for the bus, the wife told him their plans. "Coming to *Kaaneda* is our big dream fulfilled. My husband, Gaganpreet, will work here at a warehouse until we get his trucking licence, then we will open a trucking business and buy a townhome in Brampton."

I am here hating the idea of working in a warehouse while this couple is elated to get warehouse jobs. Dave's words echo in his mind: *It is all about the way you look at things.*

Curious about expenses, Jim asked Gaganpreet, "How will you manage such a huge mortgage?"

"The trucking business is a nice business," Gaganpreet responded. "You earn top dollar getting a bank loan and rent the basement. The basement money will pay for the loan to the bank. The price of houses are going up every day. We can then re-finance and buy a bigger home."

Jim nodded his understanding of their plans and said goodbye to the couple. He went home satisfied that he had a job in hand, but felt anxious about working as a warehouse labourer. Jim called his wife about the job, then laid in his bed wondering what the first day of work would be like.

CHAPTER 6
Day One

At the start of the day, all the new workers were taken into a room, coffee was served, and the operations manager gave them a welcome speech.

"Welcome to our team," the manager said. "You are the fortunate few who made it to the next level. People in the GTA are living paycheque-to-paycheque. Many others need to work two jobs to make ends meet. We pay industry's best wage rates and expect above average work in return. You will be given targets and your work will be monitored each day. If you are not able to meet the targets, we will let you go."

Easy hire, easy fire. Interesting there are performance targets for petty jobs in this country. great going, capitalism.

They were then led to their workstations and explained what they were supposed to do. At the end of the day, Jim was exhausted. *I can't work like this for a long time. I wonder how the other folks manage to do this.* Before Jim realised it though, a couple of weeks passed by, and Jim felt stuck in the warehouse job with no hope for growth. During lunchtime he sat and talked to his co-workers and routinely inquired about their life and experiences of settling in Canada. Day by day, he started feeling more insecure and depressed. *I need to talk to Dave.*

On his way back home from the bus stop, Dave saw him walking. "Hop in, Jim," Dave called out. "Let's go for a coffee. Looks like you have been working hard."

Jim buckled up in Dave's Lexus and experienced the leather upholstery. "Nice interior, Dave," Jim said as they drove off to get coffee. But Jim's face turned sad as he shared his experience. "Based on your recommendation, I started working at a warehouse. The feeling is not good. I don't like to be inside there; it is so depressing working within the four walls for 8 hours. I don't even know light or day till I come out. It's like a prison for wage gainers. I hate the job. It pays pennies and I feel it's below my value. The other day a manager at the warehouse told me that I am a spoke in the wheel. To me it seems that I'm no better than the rest of them and can be easily replaced."

"Jim, you do not get defined by what people think or say about you. You are defined by what you keep telling yourself in your mind. Observe the conversations you are having in your mind. When you observe the thought or conversation in your mind, you destroy its negative energy over you. Know that you are somebody and be confident even when you're not sure. You won't grow unless you start thinking and feeling good about yourself. Thinking is a skill reserved by the wealthy. Most people can't think good about themselves and won't reach their full potential due to their limited ability to think and grow beyond the life situations they're stuck in."

At McDonalds now, Jim grinned. "You are cheap, Dave," he teased. "I thought you would get me a Starbucks."

"I'm not cheap, I'm wise," Dave answered with a smile. "More money to save and invest, aye?"

Jim and Dave got their coffee and muffin and took a seat to continue their conversation. "What if you become a wealthy and influential man in the next five years? How will it make you feel about the present situation you are in now?" Dave asked Jim.

"It'll make me feel confident and wealthy," Jim answered, rolling his shoulders back.

"What if you will become poor and insignificant in the next five years?" Dave asked. "How will this make you feel about the present?"

"Depressed and insecure," Jim said.

"This is what is happening in your mind," Dave said, sternly. "You are looking at the negative side of things. Most people spend time thinking they are not good enough, not confident enough, unsure of what the future holds for them. When you come from such a state of mind, you create a negative attitude that will lead you into negative behaviour resulting in a negative future."

Jim looked at Dave thoughtfully. "When you start observing your thought patterns," Dave said, "and consciously choose growth-oriented thoughts, they will open opportunities you may have never imagined. Slowly but surely these growth-oriented thinking patterns will lead you to live a bright and successful future, so choose wisely!"

"Last night, I didn't get any sleep," Jim told him, "worrying about my future in this country. I often wake up at night and feel sick in the morning. I feel nauseated before I go to work. I look at my face in the mirror and see that my cheeks have sagged and my eyes are puffy. Settling in this country seems more than I can pull off. It's an ordeal to me."

"Jim, we suffer not from events in our lives but from the judgment we make about them," Dave said. "Most people live in a self-created prison of their mind. Don't be one of them."

"But my family, friends and colleagues call me from back home and ask me how life is in Canada," Jim said in reply. "And I don't know what to tell them. Should I say life sucks, or should I say I am happy to come here and do a labour job?"

"The more you beat yourself down," Dave said, "the more suffocated you will become in your self-architected prison. How does any of that matter Jim? If you alone will do all the thinking for people, what will be left for people to think about?"

"At this point," Jim said, feeling sad, "I am at rock bottom."

"This is an opportunity," Dave said.

Confused, Jim looked at Dave through teary eyes.

"Jim, you hit rock bottom!" Dave exclaimed. "The only way to go now, is up! People will think and judge you based on their internal references and filters, and they are free to do so. You know your capabilities, your potential, your success, and you know the value you can deliver to the marketplace. Make each day a litany of small achievements in whatever work you do, and soon you will be recognised for your success. Once you're able to envision a confident, influential and resilient You, people will sense it and buy into your confidence."

"I have been trying to hold on," Jim said, "but today was an exceptionally tough day at the warehouse. The work atmosphere is so demoralising. I was talking to my coworkers during lunch, and most of them have been in this country for 7 to 10 years. Various backgrounds, different countries, and all possess good qualifications. They weren't able to get jobs that suited their past qualifications and experience. In fact, one elderly gentleman told me the fate of all new immigrants is the same. Once you land here, all you can do is work in a warehouse. Another colleague chimed in 'the longer you're working a daily wage job, the slimmer your chances to get a break into the industry and field of your choice. Is this real, Dave? What if what they said became true? I get nightmares about being stuck in a menial wage job for the rest of my life."

Dave smiled. "Here is today's wisdom: the reason those people have kept working there for the past 7-10 years is because they got comfortable."

"Why would anybody get comfortable doing a laborious job?" Jim asked.

"If they were unhappy and discontented with what they did," Dave said, "they would have found a way out of that job or made a way to escape the kind of job they didn't like. Lesson two, they didn't have good references. And I caution you here … if you chose to keep them as your references, you may end up working there for a long time."

"Good to know," Jim replied, listening intently.

"Lesson three is the most important," Dave continued on. "Stay away from the naysayers. They are the ones who will keep complaining but won't do anything about it. Such people don't go far in life and you'll find plenty of them working in such jobs for years together. Understand there is no good or bad job; it is how you see it. If you look at the job as a good job, you'll never mind working there for the rest of your life. But you are ambitious, Jim. You want more than a low income, labour-intensive job at a warehouse."

"I crave more responsibility, Dave," Jim said, with conviction.

"Then stay away from people who talk negative," Dave replied. "Negative about the work, negative about the country, negative about the wages, negative about the company, the company benefits - you name it. You need to shift your focus from where you are currently to where you want to be. You need to be wise in choosing the thoughts that come to your mind. You must ensure that you don't hang out with negative people for long or else you will end up like them: broke, stupid, and sick."

"But Dave, everyone there is the same. How do I not hang out with them?"

"I'm not saying don't talk to them," Dave corrected. "Instead, limit your time of exposure to them and brainwash the negative thoughts that they may put in your mind everyday. Associate the maximum amount of your time with people you want to be like. Network with people who are doing the jobs you want to get. Buy them lunch. And most importantly, focus on the end goal in mind. Visualise in your mind securing the job you have always wanted."

"Does visualisation really work?" Jim asked. "At this point, my prayers don't go any further than above my head."

"Visualisation is a way to program your mind," Dave said. "Every morning when you get up, close your eyes and breathe, and feel the air cleaning your body, your soul, and your mind. Exhale the negativity that you may have accumulated. Do this for as long as you feel you need to. Then give thanks, be grateful for the good that you have."

"This sounds good in theory," Jim told him, "but I just don't know."

"Even if you come from a place of distress," Dave said, "there will be something good about the situation. You can be grateful for the clean air you are breathing here in Canada. You can be grateful for the good health you have, for the job that pays your bills. Being grateful is the panacea for getting what you need. When you're in a thankful state, you cannot be negative."

"I have tried meditation," Jim said, "but it doesn't work for me. This all looks good and easy to say, but doing it is not easy."

"It's easy to do," Dave countered. "It's also easy not to do it. The choice is yours. People who have achieved what they sought were able to achieve because they were ready to do the things 90% of the population would not do. Failures leave clues. Don't do the things that such people do. Once you get that, you'll be able to come out from that job you hate."

"You asked me to go there, now you ask me to come out from there, Dave?" Jim said, incredulously. "You speak from both sides of your mouth."

"You need to work there to keep the income flowing," Dave corrected him. "It's easier to keep your sanity when you have money flowing; otherwise, you'll go back home if you deplete your cash reserves. I want you to win, I want to ensure you settle here and contribute to the development of this wonderful country. Nevertheless, expose yourself to the fullness of life's experiences. Moving forward, you will realise that every experience - good or bad - is shaping who you become. Hopefully, you will use this experience as a gift for making life better for yourself and for the people around you."

"Since I had these conversations with the people at work," Jim said, "I have been reading news stories of people who came to Canada and were not able to settle themselves here. They lost all they had coming here. They have been cursing the government and the government policies for new immigrants. Also, the Canadian industry has fewer opportunities than those across the southern border."

"Every person has a different life experience," Dave said, "so don't consume their story and make it your reality. Let them share their experience. Observe, listen, and know that your story is going to be different than theirs. Don't allow their life experience to become a part of your reality."

"It's difficult for me not to listen and imbibe what they say," Jim said. "I can't control these things in my mind."

"An antidote to deal with such situations is to identify that you have negative thoughts," Dave offered. "Come into your mind through a person, an experience or any external source. Observe the thoughts that are conjuring a storm in your mind. Write down your thoughts on paper. Writing your thoughts down allows you to view them as thoughts and disconnect yourself from its negativity. Now, reflect on your past life events that can serve you as hope or inspiration. There will be similar times in the past when life seemed hopeless and a strong prayer came out from your heart, which manifested a miracle that turned things in your favour."

"Do you believe in miracles, Dave?" Jim asked.

"I believe God works for you," Dave answered. "When you have done everything right, things may go wrong. Similarly, when you may have done everything wrong, God creates miracles that sets everything right. When you shift your internal vibration from despair to hope, from fear to courage, from anxiety to joy, you will experience a power that shifts your reality and warps things toward your advantage. You need to realise that as soon as you fix your inner dialogue, your inner dialogue fixes the results you create in the external world. Even better, see or listen to inspirational music, movies or speeches."

"I don't have a lot of time to do that," Jim said. "I wake up at 7 AM in the morning, rush to catch the bus, and go work at the warehouse, then start the grind again. By the time I get home, I'm exhausted."

"I can sympathise with that," Dave said, shaking his head in agreement. "But sympathy won't get you results. I know I'm being tough on you right now, but I can give you the direction that will lead you to were you want to be. Listen to inspirational messages while you are on the bus, or while getting ready in the morning. Make effective use of your time and you will be rewarded plenty. You must do the things that most people don't to get to the results that most people won't."

"What kind of job did you have when you first arrived here?" Jim asked.

"When I came to Canada, there were not many jobs," Dave answered, honestly. "I was studying for my real estate broker's licence. I didn't have enough money to feed my family, so I took up a job at the gas station. I checked the cash register to make sure it balanced and started work. I was in charge of the gas station and the store associated with it. The owner, Durante, was from Italy. He was nice to offer me a job when I really needed it. He taught me things by leading by example. He cleaned the store himself while he taught me how to manage it. Each day, I was enthralled by his humility. I learnt how to manage the inventory, when to reorder stock, balancing the books – blah, blah, blah. This experience earned me an MBA in managing a gas station while I worked at minimum wage. I understood that if I wanted to learn to do a business, I had to start small and then expand it. Learning what worked and what didn't while I earned an income for my family, I decided to start my own business. I took out a loan and started a convenience store which I operated full time. I leveraged my real estate business by building relations with clients who frequented my store, and in the evenings, I took my clients for viewing properties. That is how I started building my wealth in Canada. Serving before being served has been my mantra and has led me to great wealth."

"That's a great story," Jim told him.

"When your internal dialogue is venomous," Dave said, "all it will breed is harm. If you keep telling yourself that you're not getting a job, you make it a reality in your mind. Your consciousness and psyche will not be able to see beyond what you allow it to. Approach your life with an open mind and possibilities will pop up all around you."

"It's hard to see beyond what is apparent around you," Jim said, stubbornly.

"Know this secret and it will allow you to control your mind," Dave said, ignoring Jim's attitude. "Whenever your mind brings negative thoughts, you say to yourself, this is the mind's chatter. I'll decide what I choose to think and paint a picture of hope, joy, and abundance knowing that I have it."

"What should I do in situations when I can't convince myself?" Jim asked.

"People don't fear success, people fear life," Dave answered. "They're unable to live life without reservations. If you're broke and think of making a million dollars, what does your mind tell you?"

"Who are you kidding, I'm thinking," Jim answered.

"Right," Dave said. "Because it's too big of a goal to digest. Especially when you're coming from the premise of scarcity. The favourable technique to get from a state of scarcity to abundance is breaking goals down into believable achievements. Say your target is to make your first million. Start by making $10 per day, then get to making $100 per day. Once you start with the aim to achieve the thinkable, your confidence in your abilities will increase. Your mental wealth gauge will reset being comfortable with earning and managing more wealth. You'll be able to push the bar in your mind and get to the next level, and the next and the next."

"I think I set my goals too high," Jim said, bluntly.

"You just got a job," Dave said. "Enjoy it! Work hard to get a promotion or look for a job that pays you $15 per hour. Invest in yourself, attend a seminar or training, go to school to improve your abilities, and become valuable to the organisations you work for. This will enable you to deliver and draw $20/hr and then $30 per hour. Once you're doing well enough to pay your bills, think about saving 10-20% of your income and investing it. Allow your money to work for you. You can invest in multiple businesses or in real estate or in the stock market. The best investment you'll make is the investment in yourself. Every time you sharpen yourself, you will improve the ability to make more money and generate revenue. This will inspire you to set bigger and better goals. There are two things that compel a person to achieve great things: inspiration and desperation. If you're driven by both, even better."

"I guess I'm afraid though," Jim said to him. "I'm afraid of not achieving the goal I have set. I'm afraid of becoming uncomfortable. I'm afraid that I won't be able to sustain the success and the progress."

"All these are rooted in your faulty beliefs," Dave said. "Unless you clear the roots of your belief system, you won't be able to bear good fruit. I'll give you a mantra for this illness: When you lead, your mind follows."

"I'll remember your words," Jim said. "We'll see if I can apply them."

"Let me drop you off at your home," Dave said, as both got up to leave McDonalds. "Let's meet again. Come to my place over this holiday weekend."

CHAPTER 7
Beliefs

It was Canada Day, a national holiday. Jim's aunt dropped him off at Dave's house. Dave stepped out on the porch to wave to his aunt.

"Thanks for mentoring Jim," Aunt Annie shouted from the car.

"My privilege in paying it forward!" Dave replied back to her while she pulled out of the driveway. "Have a seat," Dave said, after they went inside and went to their usual spot in the living room. "How have you been doing?"

"I've been doing well, paying my bills, keeping the cashflow going," Jim told him.

"You are from India," Dave started off, "so you must be aware of the proverbial three monkeys."

"Yes," Jim said. "In India, they call them Gandhiji's three monkeys."

"Let's talk about a fourth monkey," Dave stated. The four monkeys are my spin-off to this cliché instead of looking at the monkeys not seeing, speaking or hearing evil. I have changed it to the first monkey that doesn't see negative things, the second monkey doesn't hear negative things, the third monkey doesn't speak negative things."

"What about the fourth monkey?" Jim asked.

"The fourth monkey doesn't think negatively. The fourth monkey is more important than the rest of them because there are external forces that shape an individual and there are internal dialogues that shape an individual. What an individual sees, speaks, and hears externally affects their worldview. More importantly, what an individual thinks between their two ears is the biggest creator of what a person sees, feels, and experiences in real life. In continuation of our conversation the last time, you need to be very careful about what you keep thinking or talking to yourself for most of the day."

"I'm unable to control the negative emotions that come to my mind, Dave," Jim answered. "I tried hard, but my mind always goes in that direction. I know that's why you called me over to meet. My mind always creates this crazy shit up."

"I can relate to what you experience," Dave said. "It's not only you who feels this way. People strive and toil to make a living, but they don't care enough for what they think in their minds. Well, Jim, if your mind has to create something, might as well create gold rather than shit. The mind is a very good servant but a brutal master. Tame your mind to serve you, condition it to give you a response when negative thoughts arise."

"How can I do that?" Jim asked. "For the most part, I don't even realise that I've been thinking negative thoughts."

"Start with focussing on your breath," Dave said. "When you focus on your breath first thing in the morning, you are sensitising your mind and it calms your mind and allows you to connect with your spiritual core. This elevates your consciousness to a level that will be by your side when you need it the most. As you practice this often, you will observe that your mind becomes conscious and sensitive to negative thought patterns."

"What should I do when I experience a negative thought?" Jim asked.

"When you realise that your mind is thinking negative thoughts," Dave answered, "be the observer; look at the thought as a trick of the mind. When you observe the thought as a spectator, you will detach yourself from the feeling. Now you are not a slave to the mind, but an observer looking at the thought as it passes by. Practice will make you better at policing your negative thoughts. Minding the mind is a deliberate endeavour of the wise. Thought observation will give you the reigns of your mind rather than allowing yourself to immerse into the pool of an artificial experience. I recommend you read the book *The Power of Now* by Eckhart Tolle. It provides spectacular insight into how the mind affects our being and how to control thoughts. This is just the tip of the iceberg."

"So what is the tip of the iceberg?" Jim asked.

"Minding the conscious mind," Dave responded. "A bigger challenge is to know what you do not know and fix that."

Confused, Jim frowned. "The subconscious mind. It's the foundation to reprogram your mind. Imprints from life experiences become etched into the subconscious that affect who you become. How do I fix that?"

"Christie Marie Sheldon helps people uproot their subconscious abundance blocks that get engraved into the subconscious, unsuspecting of the conditions that cause the blocks," Dave answered.

"Does this really work?" Jim asked. "That's a mouthful. Sounds like hocus pocus to me."

"How will you know unless you try?" Dave asked. "That is a valid point though. It's good to be a skeptic. Don't stop there. Put things to the test to get your own answers. Most people don't get what they dream about because of their limiting beliefs. They freeze in their path thinking about what could go wrong. The majority of the people in the world think they are not enough. It's not about what people do that determines their level of success, it's what they keep telling themselves in their mind. I have always believed without doubt that I would be rich one day, and my belief has led me to manifest becoming rich."

"Are you saying that believing is a means to achieve one's goals?" Jim asked, thoughtfully.

"Yes," Dave answered. "And that is why I asked you to write down your goals. When you write your goals down and give it life, you drive your actions and your spirit in that direction. When you have the faith and take progressive action to achieve the goals, more often than not, you get the desired results. 'When you lead, your mind follows.' Can you share an experience you had in your personal life when you were absolutely certain that you would achieve a certain outcome, and it happened?"

"I participated in an essay competition and realised that the essay I was writing turned out to be so fantastic that I would win," Jim said, excitedly. "I internalised it and believed with conviction that I would win. And I won, to my surprise, the first prize."

"Exactly!" Dave said in response to Jim's achievement. "When you execute your work with a belief of certainty, most often you will find that things magically work out in your favour. There was no difference in the kind of action you or the other participants in the competition had. All contestants were writing the essay, many people had prepared themselves, but the difference that made your essay stand out was that while you were writing, you believed and emotionalized that you had already won the competition. Most people don't realise that life is more about the beliefs that mould them or break them. People strive to work hard with the hope of success and lose hope when they don't see results."

"Most people working a wage job, they work really hard," Jim said. "Still, do they get compensated as much as the owner of the company does?"

"No," Dave answered. "These people don't get paid as much. It's not because they're lazy or incompetent - rather because they don't think hard. They don't believe the abundance within them can lead them to health, wealth, and prosperity. In fact, there are numerous examples of people who rose from rags to riches when they discovered this one thing. You get what you believe - with intensity. There are many people who go out to achieve a goal and as life events happen, they give into the pressure and decide they will tolerate less than what they set out with. Now, this is a soul-damaging thought process. And over 90% of the people come from this frame of mind settle for less than what they are capable of. They allow themselves to be where they were not rising to their full potential."

"Have you ever come across a person who is making a seven-figure income and you say, hey, I'm smarter than this person?" Dave asked. "What do you think is happening here? It's all about the thought process, the beliefs in their minds. Those people believe they are the best and believe they can make that kind of money. And they do make that kind of money! Eazzzzily. Money gravitates to people who don't run after it, but who own it. These successful people get so motivated that they don't see failure as an option. On the contrary, they're comfortable with failing."

"This seems to be a contradicting statement," Jim said.

"Achievers learn from their success and failures and use those results to find their way to their end goal." Dave stated, "If you want to succeed, you have to let go of what people say or believe about you. People are going to create an opinion about you no matter what you do. It's better to be yourself and let people think what they want to think, than to fit their expectations and still have them draw their own conclusions about you. Most successful people aren't afraid of being looked down upon. They're ok with being let down and being vulnerable. At the same time, they have self respect that will not allow naysayers to crush their spirit."

"I think part of my problem is that I'm afraid of failing," Jim said, glumly.

"For the most part of our lives, we are taught that failing is a bad thing," Dave said, agreeing. "It's a bad thing if you don't "learn from the experience. But you can leverage failure to scale your success to the next level. Different things drive different people to get rich. What is the driving force that drives you to become wealthy, Jim?"

"To have a sense of security, I guess," Jim answered.

"For some, it's the fear of poverty and debt," Dave said. "That fear will drive them to take so much action. For them, broke is uncomfortable. Debt is uncomfortable, poverty is uncomfortable. Being average is uncomfortable. Mediocrity is uncomfortable. Here's another mantra: Make being mediocre and middle-class uncomfortable, change your beliefs and see what you can become. Your riches will swell beyond your current capacities of thought when you stop tolerating your own shortcomings. One thing that has helped me during tough times is to say that things are getting better each day, or things are working in my favour, or I receive help from people to get closer to my desired outcome everyday."

"Will saying these positive statements solve my problems?" Jim asked. "Seems silly."

"No," Dave responded, "but it will get your mind to be at ease and give you access to your dormant abilities to deal with the situation in style. Look at the story of Ray Kroc, the owner of McDonalds. Ray used to be a milkshake mixer salesman. Toward his old age, he was convinced about the potential of small-scale fast food that he changed the fast food industry in the U.S. and eventually the world. Colonel Sanders didn't have money for retirement and got motivated to sell his fried chicken recipe. He knew being broke was worse than being rejected 1000 times. He kept knocking on doors, getting rejection after rejection, and eventually made Kentucky Fried Chicken a stunning success."

"Back at home, I had everything," Jim said. "A debt-free condominium, a well-paid job with benefits, friends and family, an easy life. Coming to Canada has sent me back in time - like I pressed the reset button. I have other worries as well with my wife and mother managing their expenses by themselves. I'm unable to send them money from here, which makes me feel bad about myself. I feel insignificant. I need to get a good-paying reputable job soon so that when my wife comes over, we can save money and purchase a home for ourselves."

"Why do you want a home, Jim?" Dave asked.

"So we can plan to start a family," he responded.

"Why are you preventing yourself from having a child by building a hurdle for yourself?" Dave said.

"I cannot imagine starting a family without a place to live," Jim said.

"There are so many immigrant families that come to this country with kids and don't have a home, Jim."

"I'm not concerned about other people's preferences," Jim said, flatly. "I'm concerned about certain beliefs I have about how things should be before I can take the next step. At this point, things are not going according to my plan. I don't think I'll make it in Canada."

"When things go according to your plan it is good," Dave answered. "When things don't go according to your plan it's even better. Because when things aren't going according to your plan, it's going according to a plan of the divine. Believe me on this. The divine will always have a better plan than you have for yourself. This doesn't mean that you shouldn't plan. It requires you to plan even more, so that the divine can intervene and provide you the best. If there is no plan, there might not be divine intervention."

"Based on my current circumstances, I am unable to think positive thoughts," Jim said, sadly. "All I see is hopelessness and despair. I can't come to believe that I will ever be able to settle well in this country, or generate a high level of income with a decent lifestyle. Unlike you, I'm not as pumped up and motivated, especially when life is playing oddball with me."

"How long has it been since you came to Canada?" Dave said. "A few months? This is the time to remember your Why, the reason you came here. What will happen if you go back and some years down the line you or your family are unhappy with the level of pollution in your home country? Understand this: life may sometimes be a struggle. Each day there is something that is going to happen, good or bad. Once you accept that, you'll look at life with a whole new perspective."

"The good I will accept," Jim stated. "I don't want the bad stuff."

"You can't appreciate the good enough if you haven't experienced the bad," Dave countered with conviction. "Life's experiences are a blessing in disguise. They provide you with new opportunities to build character, to understand the contrast, and appreciate the good while it's there to become stronger during the tough times. It's not important to me what you believe, Jim, because what you believe is yours to believe. It's important to me what I believe and what works for me. I have discovered that by believing what I believe, my life is filled with joy and happiness. And you have discovered that by believing what you believe, your life is filled with struggle and despair. What I'm trying to explain to you is everyone gets to choose what they want to believe. Choose wisely, Jim."

"How Dave?" Jim said with despair. "What options do I have?"

"You have two options," Dave answered. "Making money work for someone else or for yourself. Work at a job or start a business."

"How can I find a business I would like to pursue?" Jim asked, with doubt in his voice.

"Seek and you shall find," Dave told him. "Ask and you shall receive. There's a seminar on real estate next week. I'll take you with me."

"How much is the fee?" Jim said.

"$550," Dave said. "I got you covered."

"Thank you," Jim replied, grateful to Dave for paying the fee. There was no way he could afford it.

"By the way," Dave said. "Did you sponsor your wife's permanent residency?"

"Yes, I submitted all the documents," Jim replied. "The file is in incubation now."

"Good luck with that, Jim," Dave said earnestly. "Let's call it a night and go home."

CHAPTER 8
Inspiration

A few days later, Jim received an email from Dave titled, *Invitation to Real Estate Summit.* Excited, Jim clicked on the link to open it. A flashing banner read, Buy your first rental property without putting a down payment. *This is interesting, lets see what's in store for me here.* Jim reached the venue on the date of the seminar and met up with Dave outside the hall. They showed their invitation passes and entered the hall. "Let's get the front row seats, Jim."

The emcee began by introducing a broker couple, Mr. and Mrs. Hassan. They started their speech and gave an introduction to the real estate market in the Greater Toronto Area (GTA).

"The real estate markets in the GTA keep growing, do you know why?" someone asked. "The Chinese investors?" another person yelled out. "Demand?" "Availability of loans?" "Scarcity of housing?" People kept shouting out responses.

"Great answers," Mr. Hassan said. "This room is filled with likeminded people. The GTA is Canada's fastest growing real estate market after Vancouver. The key driver in the GTA is a fresh influx of new immigrants. Each year, a majority of immigrants come and settle in the GTA. Even the ones that initially settle in other provinces under the provincial nominee program eventually find their way into the golden horseshoe area. This is because of jobs and money. The GTA is a key hub for business in south central Ontario. And where people, money and jobs flow, the real estate market keeps giving returns. Have you heard of a friend or family losing money in the stock market? Yes?

Have you ever heard of a person losing money in real estate? Nooooooooo!! That's it. In the stock market, the bull climbs up the stairs and the bear falls off the roof. In housing, it's different. The housing market cycles grow gradually and recede gradually. Housing is a safe bet any day."

The seminar continued. Dave and Jim stepped out for a lunch break to grab a sandwich.

"Doing business in Canada is not as lucrative as doing a business in some other part of the world," Jim stated.

"What makes you think so?" Dave responded.

"Look at the government policies," Jim started off. "They all are anti-entrepreneurial. All the odds are stacked against the business owner. An employee gets to work fixed hours and can have the rest of the time for themselves, however, the business owner needs to hustle day and night for the next client, the next meeting or the next business deal."

"Jim, you're not looking at a business the way it's supposed to be," Dave insisted. "People who think this way talk themselves out of starting a business. The fact is that starting a business in Canada is not as difficult as you think. I do acknowledge that it's not meant for everyone. Most people are happy with their 9 to 5 jobs, and that's ok. Jim, if you are unhappy with the job you're doing, you must choose between doing a low income job or building a fortune. Many immigrants who are unable to get a meaningful job in Canada often start a business. This is an alternate means to make a niche for yourself and benefit the country's economy. Nevertheless, people who have good jobs also have a side business to generate an alternative source of income. Any additional source of income that you create will help you grow your wealth while you toil hard at your job. There are multiple ways to generate a second source of income."

"Sorry to interrupt you," Jim said abruptly, "but how will I be able to manage the second source of income while I work a full time job?"

"As I explained earlier," Dave said, "you need to know WHY you need to do it. The life of every accomplished person has revolved around WHY. If you have strong reasons, you'll find the means and the time to do it. It may not be easy, but you need to become a better, smarter, and stronger person than you are now. You need to invest in yourself, to be able to liberate yourself from the vicious cycle of trading time for money. Here is what I found. As you progress and go higher in life, the easier it gets to make money."

"How is that possible?" Jim asked. "All I know is people who go higher are working harder and have the most responsibilities. And if something were to go wrong, the ones at the top lose their jobs first."

"That itself is a good reason to start your own business because you have more control over things than you do at a job," Dave responded. "Secondly, do you think the people at the top have reached there without solving problems? Haven't they created a lot of value before they reached the top? People at executive positions in an organisation solve huge problems, and that's why they sit at the top. You too can sit at the top if you make yourself capable in solving big problems. Losing their jobs is the least of their worries because if they did, they would surely get another one. They are resourceful to start their own thing and make money themselves."

"Then why don't they?" Jim asked.

"That's a good question," Dave said. "Most leaders don't do that - not because they're not capable, but because they can't see themselves doing anything different. This doesn't mean that most people in corporations should leave their jobs and start businesses! There are so many executives who are delivering the best services they can to their corporations and taking home a fat cheque. What I'm trying to say is you need to reflect and explore whether you have any gifts or talents that the world can benefit from, and use it to help people meet their needs and become wealthy. Note this Jim, not everyone feels they're living to their full potential, trading time for money."

"Then why go ahead and take the pains to start a business" Jim said, "if I eventually have to do a job? Especially when we know that running a business demands more from a person than working at a job."

"Understand this. Jim. You need to think like the rich to become rich; remember what you think about becomes your reality. If you think you can achieve it you are right, if you think you cannot achieve it, again you're right. The choice is yours. What do you want to think about? The best part is that with the existing technology and opportunities that are available to us, you can conjure a business idea and achieve it. If you want freedom or flexibility of time you can do it; if you want to work on your terms, you can do it. If you want to run a one-person show, you can. If you want to have a four-hour work week, you can. If you want to travel the world while writing a story, you can do that as well. There are no limits to what you can achieve once you set your mind at it. After all, it depends on you and what you want to achieve from life. Your beliefs are the only limit you set for yourself."

"So interesting," Jim chimed in. "But let's get back to the seminar. It's time for the session to start."

To Jim's surprise, Dave was invited as a speaker for the event. Dave went up on the stage and addressed the audience. "Thanks for coming back, everybody," he said.

"Now that you have had your fill, let me help you learn some more about real estate. Have you heard about the life stories of Ignat Kaneff and Rai Sahi? These are phenomenal examples of Canadian immigrants who have made it huge in maple country."

Dave continued on with his story. "In 1971, Sahi immigrated at the age of 24 years from India to Montreal, Canada. As he didn't have friends or family here in Canada, he had to fend for himself. Initially, he started working menial jobs unloading boxes for $1.50 an hour. He worked on improving his English, obtained an insurance licence, and eventually managed to get a job with an insurance company. He moved to Kingston, Ontario and started selling door-to-door life insurance. He didn't stop there, and worked and studied simultaneously to gain certification as a Certified General Accountant. In 1976, Sahi got a break at the Bank of Montreal (BMO) as a business loans officer, and moved his family to Toronto. Within four years, Sahi climbed up the corporate ladder becoming a business loans officer. When Sahi learned about a lucrative business offer, he pooled his money and purchased the manufacturing company. He turned the company around and flipped it to pocket a couple of million dollars."

The crowd murmured at this man's accomplishments.

Dave waited for the crowd noise to die down and finished the story of Sahi. "He then invested this moolah into a trucking company and sold that for a massive profit. Sighting an opportunity in a distressed real estate company, Morguard, Sahi bought a major stake in the company and turned it around as well. In early 2009, Morguard was trading at $16. Since the company has grown multi-fold, it's now one of the best performing real estate stocks in the country. Sahi became a billionaire. He then invested a part of his fortune in Golf clubs. What do you think about this man's life? Isn't it inspiring? Some people may say he got lucky; but one doesn't become a billionaire by luck alone. With keen intent, perseverance, and focused effort, he created value for the country and wealth for himself. I would like to take some questions from the audience now."

Jim stood up eagerly and asked, "Sir, what is the story of Kaneff? I've have seen a couple of buildings around downtown Mississauga with his name on them."

"Thank you for your question," Dave responded, and introduced Jim to the audience. "Jim is a new immigrant to Canada and I've been mentoring him." Jim smiled at the recognition.

"Ingat Kaneff arrived in Canada in 1951," Dave said, in answer to Jim's question. "When he reached Canada, he hardly had $5 with him, very little education, and poor English skills. Ingat was a Bulgarian by birth. His journey here was long, including a short stint as a market gardener in wartime Germany. He came to Canada with a dream of making it big and started working as a construction labourer in Toronto. As an ambitious immigrant, Ingat showed tremendous drive and enthusiasm. He believed that real estate was his path to becoming wealthy and influential. He saved money while he worked in construction and started a company that built a portion of Canada's housing, then grew the company exponentially over the next decade. By early 1970, Kaneff was ranked among Canada's top businessmen. Most of his projects shaped the City of Mississauga. In 2017, he was inducted as a member of the order of Canada. Kaneff's story is a living example that even without money, education, and English skills a person with belief in a dream and hard work can achieve great wealth. Ingat has been a generous, helpful person even when he was working hard on his dream. Now a billionaire, he continues to contribute part of his fortune in philanthropic activities."

Dave asked the audience, "So what did you learn from the stories of Sahi and Kaneff? It's that real estate is the business to make generational wealth, and with that, I'll leave the podium for the next speaker."

As the audience clapped after his speech, Dave stepped down from the stage and sat down with Jim again. During the next break, Jim and Dave stepped outside to get a drink. "It must have taken him a lot of hard work and perseverance for Sahi and Kaneff."

"Yes Jim," Dave answered. "The ones who became truly wealthy and successful were ready to do the things they didn't like in order to achieve a life they love to live. These people were no different than any immigrant who came to this country except they had strong reasons that compelled them to succeed. I'll give you an example of contemporary people who have moved on from working a full time job to owning a full time business. Twenty eight year-old Ryan Grant put his spare time during the week to good use and started a side hustle. He purchased items that go on sale at Walmart and ToysRUs then resold them on Amazon to pocket the profit. This is called 'online arbitrage.' In his third month of starting the business, he profited $9000. Once he replaced the income he gained from the regular job, he quit to run his business full time. What started as a hobby or side hustle is now a million dollar full time business. Ryan teaches people to replicate his success at online arbitrage. You can do the same by buying stuff from Costco on sale and reselling it online."

"Dave, this guy seems to have a good business acumen. I don't think I do."

"Who says so, Jim? Have you tried starting your own business in the past?"

Hesitantly, Jim replied, "I tried starting a home business such as Herbalife and Amway. They didn't work for me."

"That's MultiLevelMarketing (MLM)," Dave said. "Have you tried running a real business?"

"I had a small blogsite where I tried to earn affiliate commissions," Jim replied.

"What happened with that business?" Dave asked.

"I got one commission cheque worth $100 that's it," Jim answered. "I never went beyond that."

"Why did you stop after the first $100?" Dave asked, curiously.

"I didn't see the results, Dave. I thought I would make instant profits by running the blogsite but didn't."

"Jim, you look for instant gratification," Dave said. "You think short term. The $100 you made paid for a half month's worth of groceries for your self. From there, you should have set a target to get $200 per month so that it paid for an entire month of groceries. Once you had your food paid for, you could target being able to pay your monthly rent. Slowly and steadily, you would've been able to cover all your monthly expenses from your website. Sustaining a steady income for some time will demonstrate to you that you're ready to take your side hustle full time and grow it for your personal freedom."

"I agree, Dave. I gave up too early and understand what you're trying to explain."

"Another example is of eight year-old Ryan," Dave said. "Ryan, alongside his parents and twin sisters, has a YouTube channel. This kid with help from his parents leveraged YouTube videos to review toys. He started out in 2015. Slowly but steadily, the subscribers grew, and the kid created $11 million in 2017 and doubled their income to $22 million in 2018. Talk to me about business acumen and I'll prove to you that the internet doesn't need you to have business acumen. All you need is to be yourself, be disciplined, and persistent. Avoid the negative voices and you will make it. If this kid can do it, what excuse do you have left? The internet is a marvelous tool to generate a steady stream of income if you're persistent and produce valuable content that people can use. Now let's get back to the seminar."

After the seminar was over, Dave and Jim stood up to leave. "I'll drop you off at home, Jim," Dave offered.

Jim thanked Dave, grateful for his mentoring, advice, and support.

When they got in Dave's car and started driving to their homes, Dave brought up the types of businesses to consider starting. "If you're really good at what you do, you can register on Freelancer.com or Upwork.com. You work on your own terms based on your needs. Whether it's making a few extra dollars per hour or if you want to work full time from home, you can do that. Home cooking and catering is another means of income. Many people start their home business such as providing packed lunches to people. There are many professionals and individuals who rely heavily on takeout meals. Provide them a service and profit from it."

"These ideas are amazing," Jim said. "However, if I do start a business, I'll lose freedom of time. All I know is that most business owners must be on their toes 24/7. Most business fail in the first five years."

"Well who told you these things?" Dave asked. "Be careful with what you allow to believe. Fear is used as a weapon by the mighty to control the masses. With the changing corporate landscape, there is no security in jobs these days. The only security you have is in your ability to market your value."

"How will I be able to compete with the larger corporations that have more money, power and influence?"

Jim asked. "They can wipe out or change the course of the market to ruin any business."

"When most of these huge corporate giants started out," Dave answered, "there were other competitors that threatened them. Walmart had Kmart and Sears. Amazon had Walmart, and FedEx had the U.S. postal service. The visionaries that created these behemoths believed in their dream and knew what they had to offer. It proved to be of more value than most other big players in the market. If they could change the market value, so can you. Do you believe that, Jim?"

"What they achieved in one lifetime seems unbelievable to me," Jim answered.

"Start small, Jim," Dave said, pulling his car into Jim's driveway. "Make small wins as you work your way up. Each of these business magnets started small and used their small wins to build momentum and belief for massive success."

"Thanks for everything, Dave," Jim said, getting out of the car.

"Let's connect again to discuss this more tomorrow, Jim." Then Dave waved goodbye to his friend.

CHAPTER 9
Growth

Jim felt blessed that he knew an influential person who was sparing his time to coach him. He knew he was in good hands. The next day, Jim's aunt asked him to stay home for a plumber to come in and fix a drain. He called Dave to tell him. "Sorry I'm not able to come over today, so hope we can talk over the phone?" he asked, after explaining the circumstances. "I'd like to discuss more about starting a business, and let you know how grateful I am for your tutelage. And accepting me for my shortcomings."

"Of course, Jim," Dave said. "Everyone, including me, needs to be reminded where we fall short. All of these things I've shared with you are not new. Everyone comes programmed with negative information in their consciousness. It's only that we forget about our greatness because we get too indulged in day-to-day events."

"I've come to realize that if I follow your teachings," Jim said, "that I can do it too."

If you believe in yourself," Dave said, "you can do it provided you have three things:

1. The right references
2. A clear reason why you want to do it
3. The resourcefulness to improve yourself

"The thing that stops people in their tracks is when people lose everything," Dave continued on. "They buy defeat and surrender. If you don't allow losing to dishearten you, digging your feet into the sand and being in the game will eventually bring you success. Start a business that pays you upfront. Look for people just like you, who have done it before. Knowing people who have done it will give you the courage and confidence to believe in yourself."

"Why do people give up when they lose, Dave? How motivated will you be to continue your quest for wealth if you don't have money to pay your bills as compared to if you had money?"

"Having the money to be in the game will sustain most people to continue," Dave answered. "However, having money may also make people slip into their comfort zones where they keep trying and keep losing money without a deep desire to succeed. They're just throwing bets out of the window thinking that one will win them a fortune. This is like gambling in the lottery where you only bet and don't do much. As I always say, to be successful you need to bring the power of intent and amalgamate it with the power of action to reap the results of fulfilment and abundance. Nevertheless, there are others who stake everything all at once and don't surrender until they make it through to the other side. They cut all the cords and make things work for them. The interesting thing is, there is no one way to achieve what you want, and everything works differently for different people."

"Dave, what if I don't succeed?" Jim asked, earnestly. "What if my over-optimism to make it big in life is a fantasy and not a reality? What if I fail? What if I lose money?"

"What will happen is of less consequence than what you will learn and become from the experience," Dave answered. "Even if you're unable to make it big, your best shot will make you realise whether it's something you wanted to do or not. Life as I see it is all about creation – realisation – recreation."

"I see your point," Jim said, "but so much is at stake with bringing my wife here if I fail."

"Complaining and worrying are two destructive seeds of the mind," Dave said, holding up two fingers. "When you worry or complain about anything, you're wasting your time and energy. A wise man once said, 'I have a limited amount of energy in a day and I need to spend it wisely.' Don't spend your energy worrying and complaining about something. You'll end up buying it, and it will make you poorer. Instead, if you spend your time on gratitude and joy, it will help you build character. Character will enable you to build wealth, and gratitude will open floodgates of wellness and abundance."

"What about the scores of people who cannot start a business?" Jim asked. "Can they be rich, wealthy, and financially free?"

"Yes Jim, there are solutions to every problem if you search for it in the right locations."

"Dave, I thought about getting into the real estate business but I don't have enough money. The tips shared at the conference didn't resonate with me. Last night, I was reflecting and asked what do I want for myself. I need enough money to buy a condominium in cash and have a sustainable income to pay my monthly bills. This will enable me to work on projects that I am passionate about. I want to work because I like to work, not because I need to work. It will give me peace of mind and satisfaction. How do I manage to do that, Dave?"

"Where do you think the top five richest people in the world have their money?" Dave asked. "In real estate? No, a major part of their money is in their company. They own their net worth in the stocks they own."

What are you suggesting, Dave?"

"If you find a good business, you need to leverage its abilities and invest in them," Dave said. "Not everyone is good at doing a business. However, if you're smart, you can have a piece of a good business and build your net worth. You can invest in a rock star business and be a partner in the company even without doing the business. Warren Buffett, one of the largest investors in the world, has invested in good business over the years and compounded it over a time. This made him and his investors very wealthy. He is patient and disciplined in his investments and compounded profits over the years."

"That is correct, but I'm not a genius like Mr. Buffett," Jim said. "How am I to decide which companies are good companies to invest in?"

"You need to learn, Jim, when you set out to achieve a goal and are motivated, you will make things happen no matter what. Take classes, read books, and teach yourself how to invest in the markets, and learn from your mistakes."

"But most people lose money in the markets, including experienced hedge fund managers," Jim said.

"I don't deny your argument, Jim. People do win and also lose in the markets. It's because of emotion. Most people buy stocks when they're rising and sell when they're losing value. People who are unable to control their emotions, whether it be fear or greed, lose money in the markets. You have to be wise and patient."

The stock markets are risky, Dave."

"Life is not risk free, Jim. You need to learn to ensure the risks in life and you'll do well. In the words of Buffett, known as the *Oracle of Omaha*, 'Risk comes from not knowing what you are doing.' In the stock market, it's called hedging. There are different theories about the functioning of the markets. I chose to be a value investor."

"What is that, Dave?"

"In layman's language," Dave began to explain, "value investing is investing in a great company by purchasing its stock at a bargain price and holding it for the long term. Buffett, Charlie Munger, Guy Spier, Monish Pabrai, Joel Greenblatt, and Dr. Michael Burry are some of the great value investors of our time, whom I follow. Some books I recommend that you read are *The Little Book that still Beats the Market* by Joel Greenblatt, *Dhandho Investing* by Monish Pabrai, and *The Intelligent Investor* by Benjamin Graham. Ben Graham was Warren Buffett's mentor. Ben taught Warren how to buy good companies at discount prices. These books reflect the investing philosophy of most of these gurus. For the most part, investing is a bystander's business. You have to keep watching opportunities and evaluate them. You only buy when you find a great company at a bargain price, hold it long term, and divest to profit. Do this a couple of times and you'll be rich by the time you retire. Warren Buffett advises common people to invest in index funds or ETFs as they call it. These funds are a selection of good companies or bonds that help you have a balanced portfolio. People who want to be financially free but are unable to run a business can leverage the talent of those who do."

"How is that possible?" Jim asked.

"By investing in the world's largest casino," Dave answered. "The stock market. Unless one knows to gamble, one cannot make money in the stock markets. It's how you look at it, Jim. I'm not suggesting that you go and start gambling in the stock market by yourself. What you should do is identify a great player, a person who has demonstrated good results over the years and leverage their skills to help you grow your hard-earned money. The banks don't give you the kind of returns you can make in the stock market in a legitimate way."

"Who is a good investor in Canada?" Jim asked.

"You must do your own research and decide for yourself," Dave answered. "I personally follow the blog of Garth Turner – thegreaterfool.ca. He has been writing his blog for quite some time now and helped manage people's money in a sustainable manner. One such story was posted on CBC news – An IT professional couple, Kristy Shen and Bruce Leung, started saving money for a house by investing in the markets. They collected sufficient money, enough to make a down payment on a house, a few hundred thousand, and sought Garth Turner for helping them retire early, retire rich, and travel the world. With diligence, patience, frustration, and perseverance they invested their money over the years and managed to retire in their 30's. Their story is living proof that regular individuals, without business acumen, can achieve financial freedom. They call it the FIRE movement."

"And that stands for?" Jim asked.

"Financial Independence Retire Early," Dave replied. "There are two ways for median income workers to make extra money in a legitimate manner:

1. Spend less and save more
2. Make more money

"You have a limit to save money from what you earn," he said. "But there is no limit to earning more money that can enable you to save more. Start working on your plan to replace your hourly wage by the amount you earn in a day, then replace your daily income with the pay cheque you get in a week. Replicate this to make your monthly income equal to or more than your annual income. You'll find that as you expand your physical and mental capacity to be rich, you'll be able to earn every hour what you earned in a year. There is a progressive realisation of your goals one step at a time. As you grow and expand your mental wealth-stat, your income will expand." Your wealth-stat is like a thermostat. What you make to be your normal comfort level, your subconscious will get used to it and bring it to fruition in your life. So, in order to have more money, you need to increase your wealth-stat."

"Dave, I also learnt that most Canadians amass their wealth by investing in real estate."

"That is true, Jim. As you now know, I'm a realtor by profession and used to tell my clients the same thing, however, each person has their own way of growing their wealth."

"As I understand it, investing in real estate is difficult for most people with a median income," Jim said, "especially in the metropolitan cities. This is a big barrier for most new immigrants to enter the real estate market."

Dave agreed. "Yes, that is true. I should not be saying this as a realtor myself but investing in real estate requires large sums of money. Most new immigrants don't have that when they arrive in Canada, so I recommend saving a pile of cash before entering the real estate market. Spin your initial seed capital in the stock market to make a profit and use it to make a down payment on a home. Rinse and repeat."

"Is one type of stock better than another?" Jim asked.

"As a new immigrant, one can create cashflow income by investing in good Real Estate Investment Trusts (REITs)," Dave answered. "REIT Exchange Traded Funds can provide you with control over good real estate deals that are owned and/or operated by the parent company. When you have the money, you can buy a house and rent it in cities where the rent you receive equals or exceeds the expenses incurred by your house. REITs are offered by professional companies that will do the work for you at a low risk and help you make money. You don't need to fix toilets, manage the payments, beg your tenants for rent, and above all, you won't be harassed by tenants who can sue you and make money off your property. If managing tenants is something you don't want to do, investing in REITs is an easy way to earn a significant return on real estate. Remember this, Jim. Great riches are sequestered for the few in places that are unattractive to the masses."

"This sounds a like a much safer investment," Jim said, thoughtfully.

"Before you invest," Dave said, "save an equivalent sum of a full year of your monthly expenses in your savings account. As a safety hedge. It will give you peace of mind and sleep at night. Statistics show that nearly 43% people in Canada fret over the fact that they won't be able to pay their bills if they miss a pay cheque. Use conventional wisdom for unconventional results. The wise invest in distressed instruments such as stocks, bonds, real estate, land, and commodities when they're available at a bargain price. The masses buy things from stores when they go on sale but do the opposite when it comes to investing. People buy stocks, bonds, and real estate when it rises and sell when they fall; they major in minor things."

"What you shared is a millionaire's advice. Dave, what if I do everything right and things still don't work out the way I intended?"

"If things aren't going right, even after you did everything right," Dave answered, "take care to ensure you left no stone unturned. It doesn't mean you're not good at it. It's just that life is telling you, you can handle it. You're better than this. Or life is preparing you for bigger challenges. Life is testing your resolve. Once you overcome, you will see massive success. When doing things for the first time, you may feel hesitant or incompetent. People will sense you're doing it for the first time. Do it anyway. It's better to read, review, and rehearse:

1. Read about the situation you're going to be in
2. Review what you know and what you don't
3. Rehearse your strategy or approach before you step into the field

"People seldom laugh at the same joke twice," Dave said, "but they'll easily repeat depressing things in their minds. As an entrepreneur, you need to learn to refocus your thoughts and mind in a direction away from the problems and focus on the results."

"Thanks for your guidance, Dave. I'll keep that in mind."

"So how has your wife's PR sponsorship progressed?" Dave asked.

"That's a concern," Jim said, looking worried. "It's been eight months now. I still don't see the light at the end of the tunnel. I'm running out of patience and so is my wife."

"Well, Jim, whatever happens, happens for a good reason. Life is giving you time to settle down before your wife arrives. Take care."

"You too, Dave."

Jim hung up the phone. He looked up at the ceiling to clear his thoughts, pursed his lips, and took a deep breath. In his mind, he visualised getting a job with a decent salary.

CHAPTER 10
Giving

Jim got into a routine while he was being coached by Dave. His interactions with him gave Jim the moral support and encouragement to continue his pursuit of settling in Canada. While Jim's friends reached out to him for information regarding immigration to Canada, Jim himself was challenged to fit into the culture and the country. Jim called Dave to obtain insights regarding some of these conversations. "The other day, a friend of mine contacted me because she plans to immigrate to Canada."

"What did you advise her?" Dave asked.

"I warned her about the challenges in Canada," Jim answered. "I have been going through my own set of challenges and don't want her to bear the same hardships."

"Jim, what you call hardships will be another person's opportunity. Try not to influence your negative views on your friend. Give her a realistic picture of what to expect when she comes to Canada. Let her decide her purpose to come and live here. What if she becomes the next Sahi or Kaneff? Instead, you can mentor her to equip herself with the skills that will empower her to integrate into the Canadian society with ease. Ask her to come well prepared before arriving and to complete an online e-course from a recognised Canadian institution or a certification program related to their field."

"But Dave, completing an educational program before arriving may prove to be expensive due to the Forex conversion."

"Would you want your friends to have a better chance to succeed, or think about expenses?" Dave said.

"Having a Canadian education or certification will increase their chances of securing a job in Canada. There will still be some who will not be able to afford these expenses. Advise friends who come here without a Canadian education that if they plan to obtain a student loan for a course or program, it may delay their settlement. Borrowing a student loan will get them into debt. Studying and working simultaneously proves to be challenging for many new immigrants. Anyway, if they do end up taking a course or certificate program, they should ensure that the program has a co-op placement. Programs that offer co-op placements increase the probability of getting a job. Oh!" Dave said abruptly. "This conversation gave me an epiphany. This could be your path to fortunes in this country."

"Are you suggesting something, Dave?"

"Yes, you could become an immigration lawyer," Dave said. "Since you have the experience of immigrating, most of your friends and family will seek your advice to come here. You can get paid for giving immigration advice. Another idea is to help new immigrants get a credible job. The problem you faced when you came to Canada is a big problem, and the person who can figure out a way to solve it will create massive value for the industry, new immigrants, and themselves. This in turn will make them rich."

"That's a great idea," Jim said to him. "There's a steady market of new immigrants and the business is lucrative." Jim snapped his fingers and smiled. "When you program it well, the subconscious will provide you with ideas."

"Talking about the subconscious reminds me of something," Dave said. "How much money have you donated in the past ninety days?"

"None," Jim answered. "Why would I bother to donate money? Especially when I'm on a tight budget."

"Generosity unlocks the floodgates of abundance, Dave said. "Here is another million-dollar value advice. Start with 1 %. When you give away 1% of the money you earn, it sends a subconscious signal to your mind that you have more than enough money to help others. This act of generosity opens floodgates of abundance."

"So I can start my donation when I have my million, Jim said, cleverly.

"Haha!" Dave chuckled. "My friend, if you can't give a nickel out of a looney, forget giving a thousand out of a million. You need to start when the amounts are small. When you're in charge of the small things and manage them correctly, you will be entrusted with larger things in life."

"Why is it that one part of society has to toil hard and others needs to pay taxes to fund free food, housing, and facilities for the lazy?" Jim asked, in a serious tone.

"Hmm," Dave uttered. "I see you're seeking bottom line benefits in paid taxes. That is not a bad thing. What you need to understand is that we're all humans and need to care for other human beings."

"I'm surprised that you as a capitalist are saying this, Dave."

"You will find that most capitalists are generous and do more than people think," Dave answered. "Most wealthy people donate resources in their own accord. The government oversees everyone and steps in to help when it identifies human atrocity. Canada has always been known as a benevolent nation bringing respite for the underprivileged and unfortunate individuals. Being selfish doesn't create synergies."

"What about the terrorist and insurgents that sneak into our country under the shelter of being refugees?" Jim asked.

"Leave that to the authorities to deal with," Dave said. "Metaphorically, if a farmer starts trying to chase away the birds, they will lose sight of the crop. As an individual, your focus should be to create value for others so you can generate wealth for yourself and your country. Over the years, what I have learned is that there will always be two sides to any argument. I like to support the side of the house that favours an inclusive approach that benefits the masses by giving."

"I don't feel I'm in any position to donate right now," Jim said.

"Giving is the beginning of receiving," Dave said. "If you study most wealthy individuals, you'll identify that all of them started from a premise of gracious giving. They look to contribute to a cause greater than themselves. If you're selfish and only look to benefit for yourself, you may not get far ahead in life than what you have desired. If you go forth and help people with their mundane lives, you will be touched by the experience and it will inspire you to do more, grow more, and give more. The more you give the more you will grow. The more you grow the more you will be able to give; this momentum will build itself up into an upward spiral. And even if you don't get anything in return, remember that your life is not about what you have accumulated, but how. It's about what you contributed to the society. Giving never goes unrewarded. If you keep giving, the divine will always look after you, take care of you, and ensure you're doing well in life. When you demonstrate benevolence by giving, an unfathomable power comes to your service. You'll see things transpire in a magnificent way. Hurdles that have clogged your wheels will release themselves, making way for results and progress."

"I struggle to settle in Canada," Jim answered to Dave's lecture. "I'm unable to get to that frame of mind. I feel I'm the one who should be on the receiving end rather than the giving end of the table."

Dave smiled. "Jim, are you even hearing what you just said? How do you expect to become successful and wealthy when you function from a place of scarcity? When you want to be on the receiving end, you're already becoming a needy person. If you get yourself into a position for giving, you're functioning from a place of abundance. Things you need will come to you as you continue to give to others."

"How do I make that shift, Dave? How can I function from a place of abundance? Because at the present, I only see a scarcity of opportunity."

"Practice gratitude everyday, Jim. Gratitude is the secret that will lead you to great wealth and riches. When you start from a place of gratitude, you will realise that more of the good stuff will flow to you freely. Complaining about what you don't have will restrict all the good from flowing to you. Complaining locks you in a dungeon where you isolate yourself from receiving the freedom life has to offer. Use your mind as a servant; don't let it enslave you. You can choose abundance or you can choose scarcity. Do you want to have freedom of time and money or do you want to work in a laborious job?"

"Dave, my job just pays the bills for now. I don't have any interest in working at the warehouse. I have to motivate myself every day to get out of bed and go to work."

"Well then, Jim, I wish that you may lose your job."

"Why would you say something like that?" Jim asked, in horror.

"Well, Jim if you don't like your job, it's better not to have it."

"My job pays the bills," Jim said, flatly, a little irritated with Dave at this suggestion.

"Interesting!" Dave said, brightly. "I see someone suddenly finds their mundane job valuable."

"Of course, I do," Jim exclaimed. "I wouldn't be able to survive this without it."

"Son, you need to be thankful that you have a job," Dave said. "Years ago when I came to this country, it was hard to even find a labour job. Things were much harder back then. When you remove the job out of your life, you realise it has a purpose and you approach it from a place of thankfulness rather than complain. Gratitude is the gateway to grace. And grace leads to wealth. Be thankful for what you have and work towards what you want to achieve. This will allow an abundance of opportunities to flow to you."

"After, I have practiced gratitude on a daily basis," Jim asked, "what are the next steps that I have to take to be successful?"

"Most people are in different stages of their personal lives," Dave said. "You need to identify where you are and start from there. Even if it means to start small and growing steadily. Allow yourself to get wealthy. Most people are the biggest barrier between their dreams and their success. Results are a product of thought and action, and if you look for limitations, you'll find more of them. If you look for opportunities, you will find plenty. There's one more thing that blocks abundance from flowing to people. We'll explore this when we meet again in person."

"Yes, I'll look forward to that," Jim said.

"Now go, set an example for your friends by working on your dream list," Dave concluded. "Create abundance for yourself and your friends. And let me know about the results you produce."

"Thanks Dave, will do, and talk to you soon." Jim hung up the phone and reflected on this latest conversation with Dave.

Having been mentored by Dave, Jim leaned more on the idea of starting his own business than trying to look for a well-paying job. He knew that with Dave's guidance, he would succeed at anything he aspired.

Jim replaced his goal of getting a well-paid job to creating a business generating over $100,000 per year.

CHAPTER 11
Forgiving

Jim and Dave didn't talk for a quite a few months. This caused Dave concern, so he went over to Jim's house to see if he was home. As it turned out, Jim had been in his room sitting quietly.

When Jim answered the door, Dave boisterously said, "You still alive?"

"How are you?" Jim said in greeting.

"I'm good, but you don't seem very good today, Jim."

"I wanted to share an experience that has been eating me from within," Jim said.

"Why didn't you call me?" Dave asked, as they both sat down at the kitchen table.

"I didn't know how to tell you," Jim answered. "As recommended by you, I took classes toward obtaining my licence to work as an immigration lawyer while I continued working at the warehouse. I toiled hard with work and study, and I eventually got my licence."

"How does it feel?" Dave asked.

"I feel good about the licence," Jim said, "but not so good of the experience."

"Tell me more," Dave said, now a bit concerned.

"I befriended a smart guy, Manish, while attending immigration classes," Jim started. "He came from India and we planned to partner together to start an immigration consulting firm. He had a wealth of contacts in India and the Middle East who were interested in migrating to Canada. I offered the technical expertise and skills to formulate the best avenue to process their immigration files."

"Okay," Dave said. "Go on."

"We started a business from our homes," Jim said, "and he would send me the details of the clientele and I would develop their application package. We had planned to split the profits 50/50. The applications started pouring in. We were charging a consulting fee of $1000 to process each application, which was much lower than the fees charged by established consultants in India and the Middle East. I also funneled in people I knew to obtain our services. This drew a large number of prospective applicants to consult with us. As the business grew, we hired four college students to help us with the application and fee processing. Our business was flourishing. I quit my warehouse job and was working full time on my business. This was the first time in life that I felt truly accomplished. I remembered your words and mentoring that led me to reach this level of success. The processing of the fees and finances were dealt with by Manish and his team. Recently, I came to know from one of my friends who recently arrived in Canada that Manish had started charging $1500 per application instead of $1000 without informing me and was embezzling my money. Nevertheless, I also learned from staff that he started a parallel organisation and processed entire files of clients by leveraging his team. I put in hard work day and night to ensure excellent customer service which led to the success of the business. I felt cheated because of him. I don't know how to deal with this. Should I sue him or should I leave amicably?" I strongly feel I should sue him and obtain my rightful share."

"I acknowledge the fact that what Manish did to you is unethical," Dave said, slowly. "At the same time, I would say that you are as much responsible as he is."

"Why Dave?" Jim asked. "Because I trusted him?"

"As an entrepreneur you always should be watching every aspect of your business," Dave said. "You are a humble person. Don't let your humility be a reason for others to exploit you."

"I can either be humble or shrewd," Jim said, in a tired voice. "I can't be both, and I chose to remain the way I am."

"Then why do you want to sue Manish?" Dave asked.

"I seek my rightful share from him," Jim answered, "and I no longer trust him that he will share truthfully."

"What is the status of your business currently?" Dave asked.

"I have not been going to work for a week and we have not been talking with each other," Jim answered. "He has been managing our clients currently."

"You see Jim, when you leave the playing field, you have already lost the attention. He is leading the game just by the fact that you have given up and accepted defeat. Did you ask him why he did something like that?"

"Yes," Jim answered. "He was indifferent and said, 'It was an opportunity I wanted to monetize.' He was afraid I wouldn't agree. He was in need to send money back home for treatment of his brother's cancer."

"Jim, I suggest you go back and work out an amicable solution with Manish to continue the business. Most communication problems occur due to misunderstandings. There are two things that drive people to do unethical things – Need or Greed. His motives seem to be driven by need. I don't mind reconciling with a person who may have acted unethically out of need. One can be tolerant to need, but not greed."

"I feel uncomfortable to go talk to him, Dave. I can't get myself to trust him moving forward."

"I hear you Jim, such times are not easy. I had a similar experience during my initial years as a new immigrant in this country. I was working hard to move from settling to thriving. While I was preparing for my realtor's licence, I started a small side hustle. I rented a van and drove around the neighbourhood to collect junk left on the streets. I carefully selected items I could refurbish. I hauled the stuff home, repaired it, and resold it to pocket a profit. The only cost I incurred was the rental for the van, the gas, and cost of fixing items. I started making a side profit with this part time gig. As I saw the inventory scale up, I needed more storage space. I introduced my close friend to the business idea and offered to pay him a commission for using his garage as a temporary storage. My friend got super excited, and we teamed up to jointly bring in the junk. Our efforts multiplied, increased the returns, and business picked up. We jointly began making an additional $2000 per month each. Looking at the immediate gains, my friend thought that he was not being paid a big enough commission for using his garage and decided to break away and start his own business. Without informing me, he incorporated a business in his name and started a franchisee to resell junk. He used my idea to build a business model for himself that he used to monetize by developing a franchisee. He blankly told me that he had started his own business and could no longer help me. I felt helpless and didn't know what to do. I was in similar situation as you are in now."

Jim listened to Dave intently and could relate to his experience. "I could have sued him and made a small fortune," Dave continued, "but instead, I wished him well and focused on my real estate business. Over the years, it grew and I made a fortune. Karma stepped in to make things straight. My friend who cheated me eventually drove the business into the ground and went bankrupt. Remember this, as much as you want to make money, never let greed drive you to justify immoral gains. Out there, karma is watching. Having said that, I'll put on my mentor's cap and ask, what did you learn from this life experience?"

Jim, with a heavy heart, said, "I feel people are selfish, they are greedy, and cannot stand to see you succeed!"

"Are all people like that, Jim?"

"At this point, I feel everyone is selfish, Dave. Everyone is only concerned about how much money they can make and how they can cheat others and grow their riches while the honest people bear the brunt of their ruthlessness. I feel this world doesn't allow honest, simple people to be able to thrive and make money honestly."

"Let me put it this way, Jim. What is the positive thing you learned from this experience?"

"All I learned is to not trust anybody in this world," Jim said, defiantly. "Life is unpredictable, and I need to be very careful with any undertaking I initiate. I should have documented the terms in black and white so that I was in a controlling position for the business model. I should have not even partnered with him in the first place. I should have known better."

"Do you have a piece of paper and pen?" Dave asked. After Jim handed him a blank sheet and pen, Dave started writing. "Here are your key lessons you learned from this experience," Dave said, and handed Jim the paper:

> 1. You need to ensure you have a lawyer, not only to guide you, but your business as well. This will protect you from threats internally and externally.

2. Know who you are getting involved with and develop an acute understanding of trustworthy people.

3. Just when things start to look good, sometimes unexpected things happen, so anticipate and be prepared for the worst.

"This experience itself is a testament that you are learning and growing," Dave said. "These experiences of life will make you doubt your own capabilities. Gather yourself together, Jim, shake off the negative, and move on."

"How do I move on when life throws hurdles at me right when I want to make things happen?" Jim said, still somewhat frustrated with his own situation.

"By clearing your mental blocks," Dave said. "These hurdles that you experience are life's way of showing you your insecurities and your inner inhibitions that are stopping you from progressing. It may sound esoteric here, but there is truth to what I am sharing. When things on the outside don't seem to go your way, look inside. When you clear the inner resistance, you'll find that the external world will take care of itself."

"How do I clear my inner blocks, Dave?"

"There are many ways to do so, Jim. Meditation is one way. Every morning when you wake up, start your day and spare the first 5 to 10 minutes to refocus your mind to the good there is in your life. Give gratitude for all that you have and all the wonders life has done for you. Look back in time and remember the blessings that have come your way, especially when you needed it the most. Life or God or whatever you choose to call it always has your back. It wants you to grow and evolve into your best self. You are not alone! God is on the lookout to make your life worthwhile. Know that that invisible presence is taking care of you and your actions. It is this divine gift that everyone of us has access to if we wish."

"How do I access it?" Jim asked, with interest.

"By being present, by meditating and centering yourself and connecting to your core being," Dave answered. "Every night before you rest, ensure you spare a few minutes to say thanks for all the good there is in this world and you will see things transform around you. What you will give out you will get back. I call it life's boomerang effect. If you give out praise, thanks, gratitude, hope, love, joy, peace, you will see these multiply in your experience. At the same time, if you emanate fear, doubt, anger, hatred, jealousy, resentment, greed, dissatisfaction, you will also see these multiply in your experience."

"But, Dave, how should I overlook the negative in my present moment and be thankful when things around me don't warrant having anything to praise?"

"If I were to ask you about five things you can be thankful about right now," Dave answered, "what would you say?"

Jim grabbed the sheet of paper and pen and wrote down the five things he was thankful for:

1. I have a loving family
2. I have you to mentor me through these struggles of life
3. I am healthy and alive with a fully functional body
4. I have a roof over my head and food to eat
5. I can act and change things

"That's all you need, Jim," Dave said, after reading Jim's answers. "If you focus well, you'll be able to identify many more things to be thankful for than you'll find negative. What you focus on, you magnify; what you ignore, you eliminate. We humans are wired to focus on the negative, Jim! That's why I say to meditate daily. And you have to forgive your friend."

"Why should I forgive him?" Jim said, indignantly. "He cheated me."

"Jim, it's not about him. It's about you. If you hold resentment against him, you are creating a block within yourself that will prevent you from attaining the good things in life. You need to care for your inner peace and you cannot be at peace without forgiving him."

"I don't want to talk to that person," Jim sniffed.

"That is completely ok," Dave said. "Close your eyes and in your mind mention that you're forgiving him and ask forgiveness from him."

"Why should I ask forgiveness from him?" Jim asked. "I didn't wrong him."

"That is what you think," Dave said, chuckling. "He may not think the same way, and when you forgive each other in your mind, you have reconciled for both of you."

Jim closed eyes, took a breath, and said, "I forgive you, Manish. Please forgive me." It didn't seem to connect initially.

"Jim, repeat this again seven times."

After Jim had done this, he opened his eyes. "How does it feel?" Dave asked.

"I feel lighter and free," Jim said, amazed.

"You also need to forgive yourself," Dave said. "I see that you beat yourself up unnecessarily for things that happen in your life."

Jim again closed his eyes and repeated, "I forgive myself" seven times. Jim opened his eyes.

"How are you feeling now, Jim?"

"I feel peaceful," Jim said, satisfied.

"That's what forgiveness does," Dave said. "It gives you freedom in your mind, in your heart, and in your soul. You won't be able to move on with life and do the things that lead you to becoming a better human without forgiveness. Because at the end of life, all the money and all the possessions are not going to come with you. It's who you become and how you contribute to people on this planet is what will remain as your legacy. Now go ahead and reconcile with Manish. You could ask him to give you your share and part with him, or you could choose to continue building your business with him. I leave the choice with you."

After Dave left, Jim though saddened by the past decided to go talk with Manish. They ended up having a soulful conversation about Manish's brother and his ill health. Manish was touched by this gesture and apologised for what he had done. They both decided to stay friends and split the business profits, but in the end, Jim declined taking his share because Manish truly needed the money more than he did.

A few months later, Jim received good news about his wife Helen's sponsorship visa. Jim thought, *When we humble ourselves, life gives us the best of things*. He went on to start his immigration consulting business. He had to share these new developments with Dave.

CHAPTER 12
Success

"Hi Dave," Jim said when Dave answered the phone, "and before I say anything else, two great things have happened."

"Tell me," Dave said, excitedly.

"My wife got her PR visa," Jim said, proudly.

Dave smiled broadly. "Congratulations!" he said. "Finally, your hard work is paying off. What's the second good news?"

"Dave, I started an immigration consulting firm. I posted a profit of $20,000 in the first 3 months."

"Wonderful!" Dave exclaimed. "It's time to celebrate! This is your next step to making a fortune. Remember, profitable sales are better than a salary. So, what is the next step?"

"I do have friends who plan to immigrate here," Jim told him. "I'm convinced that I can rebuild a client base from Asia and the Middle East. I have also learned to tap into the local market by providing ancillary immigration services to people living here. People having work visas, desiring to obtain a residency, spousal and family sponsorships, and students aspiring to obtaining Permanent Residence in Canada. I'll also be able to generate referrals back in Asia and the Middle East by building my clientele here."

"Sounds like a plan, Jim."

"However," Jim cautioned, "I need to reach out to these customers here in Canada."

"How do you plan to do that?" Dave asked.

"I plan to start a YouTube channel to educate people regarding immigration and start an online podcast," Jim said, breathlessly. "Hooo! But I feel butterflies in my stomach."

"Jim, now that you have identified your calling, it's your obligation and duty to go forth and spread the information you have. If you hold onto it, you're doing a disservice to yourself and everyone around you by your inaction. You need to bring value to the public. Share your expertise so they can make Canada a home for themselves."

"I'm confident that I will do well," Jim said. "But, sometimes my old self kicks in and makes me feel insecure. I don't know what people will think about me. What if I fail?"

"Jim, don't worry what people say about what you do. That's your gift to the world. What the world thinks about you must not stop you from doing what you are meant to do. What if Jeff Bezos or Elon Musk cared what people thought about them when they were starting Amazon and SpaceX? If you're content with what you deliver to increase value in the world, the world will be a better place. Don't let other's opinions about you steal your glory."

"I've been really good about removing negativity with meditation," Jim said, "but it's reared its ugly head again for some reason."

"If people say something negative about you," Dave started, "it could be due to multiple reasons:

A. They could be having a bad day
B. They may be insecure about the way they feel about you
C. They are just that way

"Your thoughts are an indication of the fear within," Dave said. "Doubt is the root of fear. Doubts generate fear, and fear feeds on your life force and compels you to act in a way that is not your true self. You're unable to live to the fullest. Fear only arises from associating yourself to the source by focusing on what could go wrong. Ambition provides opportunity and difficulty. Difficulty can breed fear if you allow it to, and fear will freeze your ambitions and dominate your life. Do you want fear to dominate your life?"

"Absolutely not, Dave," Jim said.

"You have to decide whether you want to survive or thrive," Dave said. "Aspiration leads to challenges, and challenges bare problems. Problems and fears coexist. And once you have overcome your problems, you grow."

"I've felt fear throughout this process and handled it," Jim said, "but the fear of what other people think has me stumped."

"The antidote for fear is to nip it while it's small," Dave answered. "If you take yourself too seriously, you'll remain fearful. Learn to joke about yourself and make things flexible for yourself. You cannot leap into the worst situation and beat yourself down. Practice and build your muscle to overcome fear. Mankind's great gift, imagination, is also mankind's greatest curse. People suffer more often due to their mental constructs than because of reality. You're doing the same thing, Jim. Be careful how you use your imagination. It could create resistance instead of success."

"This all makes sense," Jim responded.

"Imagine that you're giving an amazing speech and people are enthralled," Dave said. "They're cheering, clapping, hooting, and giving you a standing ovation. Imagine people are coming and thanking you for changing their lives for the better. How does this image look in your mind?"

"It feels exciting, Dave."

"You need to live and breathe this excitement," Dave told Jim. "I call this 'imagineering.' It means to engineer images you desire in your mind's eye. Start using fear as an ally rather than an opponent and you'll be able to move and achieve great things. Use fear as an indicator of an area that you need to improve or master. And know this: you don't need to conquer every fear. You only need to overcome fears that are blocking you from proceeding in life. When you work out all possible options to deliver results, you'll be able to overcome fear. The best way to deal with fear is to practice in the mental gym. Turn around fear into something productive. When you get a thought about something that makes you fearful, think about it as a creation of the mind. When you observe this as a thought, you detach yourself from it. Now imagine that the fear is streaking through your mind as a shooting star and sparking a wish for you. Turn the thought around and think about it in your favour. I have personally found imagineering very helpful. When I'm faced by a challenging situation, I reprogram my subconscious by repeating with emotion, visualization, and intensity the final outcome I want to achieve. When you visualise, speak, hear, move, and listen to the things you desire, you shift your focus and create your destiny."

"Sounds like I have more mental exercises to do," Jim said. "And work harder to run my business."

"Starting this business is a seed implanted in you," Dave said. "You act as an instrument for the goodness of the divine to shine through you. It's not about you; you are the channel that is being used to deliver goodness. You need to offer your gifts so they multiply. By keeping your gifts to yourself, you're sabotaging your abundance and the abundance of the many who are unable to hear the good news you bring to them. You need to be the evangelist, if this thought has come to you. You've been bestowed with the mission to serve. Having said all this, I have some important lessons for you to take home. When you do start your mission to preach, keep these things in mind:

1. You need to feel strongly about your message before you deliver it. You should have goosebumps while you're sharing your message. There is more that is communicated through feelings than there is through words that are articulated into a good speech.

2. You don't need to worry what people say about you or your speech. You are a channel of information and you are helping the divine to act through you. Offer yourself as an instrument.

3. Prepare yourself to get comfortable with negative feedback and people who will pull you down and discourage you. Most often they won't, but you don't need to worry about the naysayers as far as you're executing your mission.

4. Your internal compass will give you the fulfilment while you do this stuff. You'll be charged to go do the next seminar and the next and you'll gain momentum.

5. Start with a small group. Start small and then scale it up; in fact, if you're doing a great job, the scale-up will self-execute.

Rejuvenated by Dave's teachings, Jim consciously began monitoring his thoughts. When a negative thought would pass through his mind, he would say to himself, *This is a trick of the mind. I look at this as a thought.* While he observed the thought pass by, he detached himself from the artificial reality his mind was creating. This made him live life with a sense of control with the belief that no matter what happened, he would be able to manage the situation. He realised that most of the experiences he went through were a reflection of the decisions and thoughts he kept in his mind, and that he could alter his reality by shifting his focus.

Learning from Dave, Jim set out to experiment with his acquired skills. He created a video blog. News about him started spreading. He also approached community centers and volunteers to share his experience as a new immigrant on a volunteer basis. The community centers, though skeptical at first, considered giving him a chance. The day of his first public seminar arrived. Nervous but motivated, Jim walked into the room where new immigrants were waiting to hear his words of wisdom.

Life is about giving, he reminded himself. *Fear is your friend. What is the worst that could happen? Evaluate how you would handle the worst. Once you can handle the worst, you can go ahead and achieve your reality.*

Jim closed his eyes and took a deep breath saying internally, "I inhale courage", and exhaled saying, "I exhale fear". He continued, "I inhale peace and release anxiousness". "I inhale hope and release helplessness". "I inhale joy and release sadness". "I inhale flexibility and release stiffness". "I inhale fun and release boredom". "I inhale vitality and release lethargy". "I inhale confidence and release doubt".

Jim stood up flexed his arms and stretched for a few minutes. He opened his eyes, realising that he had the power to change things that were in his control.

Jim walked to the front of the room and began his speech.

"I stand here today because of FEAR. When I say fear, I am here not because I'm afraid, but because I don't want fear to limit me. As I start this speech, my hands are trembling, my throat is going dry, and I'm having an adrenalin rush. I want to drive fear in the corner and bring out comfort from that same corner. And I want to help you overcome your fears and help you settle in Canada."

The crowd looked appreciative that Jim was being so transparent with them. He continued on with his speech.

"Like most new immigrants, when I came to Canada, I had my own set of fears, limiting beliefs, and challenges. I couldn't come to terms with the fact that although I had an amazing education, I had to start working at the bottom. Not by choice but by necessity. I applied for jobs at multiple organisations and received no response from any of them. I was frustrated, depressed, sick to my stomach, and tense. Can anyone relate to this?"

Many audience members raised their hands or nodded their heads in agreement.

"This is a common experience most new immigrants face," Jim said. "However, I am here to share my secrets that helped me overcome my challenges and survive, learn, and thrive in this country. Many immigrants who come here with an aspiration to settle in Canada, unfortunately, go back to their country defeated by the initial challenges. Some come back again to give themselves a better shot. Some go back the second time. Some never return. What makes the difference between immigrants who stay and thrive versus immigrants who go back dejected by the challenges?"

People from the crowd started shouting out answers. "Canadian work experience?" "Hard work?" "Networking?" "Volunteering!" "Contacts!" "A Canadian education?"

"This is an engaging crowd," Jim replied, smiling. "I'm pleased with your answers. While all of these help a successful immigrant in this country, the only thing that differentiates successful immigrants from unsuccessful ones are their mindsets."

ABOUT THE AUTHOR

Mariorafols (Mario) Menezes migrated to Canada in 2015. Having experienced the typical immigrant challenges when he arrived, Mario went from a minimum wage job to creating a successful career drawing a six-figure income.

His resolve is to ease the unpleasant experiences of newcomers to Canada and support them to find meaningful   employment in their respective professions. Mario mentors newcomers to settle and thrive in Canada.

BOOK RECOMMENDATIONS

Arrival Survival Canada: A Handbook for New Immigrants by Nick and Sabrina Noorani.

Unshakeable: Your Financial Freedom Playbook by Tony Robbins

7 Strategies for Wealth & Happiness: Power Ideas from America's Foremost Business Philosopher by Jim Rohn

The Dhandho Investor: The Low-Risk Value Method to High Returns